WALKING WITH CAVEMEN

John Lynch and Louise Barrett

WALKING WITH CAVEMEN

EYE-TO-EYE WITH YOUR ANCESTORS

Foreword by Nigel Marven

First American Edition, 2003
00 01 02 03 04 05 10 9 8 7 6 5 4 3 2 1

Published in the United States by
DK Publishing, Inc.
375 Hudson Street, New York, New York 10014

By arrangement with the BBC

Library of Congress Cataloging-in-Publication Data is available for this book.
0-7894-9775-1

Produced by
HEADLINE BOOK PUBLISHING
A division of Hodder Headline
338 Euston Road, London NW1 3BH

Designed by designsection
Illustrations by Hardlines Ltd
Special photography by David Gur and Peter Georgi
Photoshop work by Jenny Bowers and Tim Goodchild
Printed and bound in Great Britain by Butler and Tanner

www.headline.co.uk
www.hodderheadline.com

See our complete product line at
www.dk.com

Contents

Preface by John Lynch

"Walking with Cavemen" is the third in a series of television productions that have brought the prehistoric world to life. After the success of "Walking with Dinosaurs" and "Walking with Prehistoric Beasts," produced by the BBC Science Unit, it seemed clear to me that our new adventure into the past should be to the next stage in the evolution of life: to the creatures that marked our human origins. The production follows the epic journey from ape to us and, through the drama of the daily lives of creatures long-extinct, it reveals the forces that shaped who we are, uncovering the unique features that make us human, glimpsed as each one emerges in the bodies and minds of our ancestors.

Telling the story presented an immense technical challenge. The human mind has evolved to recognise a fellow human instantly, and no computer animation can fool us that it is a "real person." Instead, the television production team, led by Richard Dale and Peter Georgi, developed highly sophisticated makeup and prosthetics to convince us that human actors were really ancestral ape-men. The result is an extraordinary set of images that conjure up our past. In this accompanying book we have delved even deeper into the thrilling detail of our ancestry, and it has been a privilege to write it with Louise Barrett, who kindly accepted my invitation to be the co-author of this exploration of our human story.

Foreword by Nigel Marven

My eyes hurt from the glaring whiteness. It couldn't be a snowfield – sweat trickled down my neck as a tropical sun baked the African salt pan. There was no shade, and the temperature was over 110°F. Dark shapes shimmied and wobbled on the horizon as if a mirage but there were creatures coming over the gleaming salt toward me. A hunting party of animals, strangely familiar but unlike anything I or any other human had seen before: our ancestors. To find them I'd traveled back through time about 1.5 million years. They materialized out of the heat shimmer, a group of four males and an older female.

They were lean, long-limbed, and smooth-skinned just like me, but then a young male noticed me; running forward, he grabbed one of his companions gesticulating toward me. Now this group of protohumans showed their wild animal side, inhuman guttural sounds rolling off their tongues and their faces chilling me to the marrow. The creatures advanced toward me, now so close that I could see the whites of their eyes. This seemingly insignificant feature was a crucial step on the journey to becoming human. The alarming encounter was cut short by a familiar word – "Cut!"

Director Richard Dale and series producer Peter Georgi smiled – another cracking "take." When I forgot about the film crew, the prehistoric world they'd created in South Africa was so real I often felt I really was with our apemen ancestors. The actors became the creatures after a four-hour makeup process where they had to endure prosthetics attached to their faces. My role was as the host of the television series to guide the viewer through the story of our own evolution.

John Lynch, author of this book, was on set. He told me that *Homo ergaster*, the creatures that had just been filmed, were probably the first of our ancestors to walk out of Africa. All of the fossils ever found of the lineage that leads to modern humans would fit easily into the back of a Landrover. There can sometimes be controversy about the interpretations of their finds, so in writing this book John has found a consensus about our evolutionary story.

Co-author Louise Barrett lends other special skills to this study of our ancestors; she looks at their cousins and ours still alive today. Many ideas of how our ancestors lived rely upon comparative studies of monkeys and apes living in the wild today. I was with Louise for another documentary on a masterclass on how to speak baboon, with just my face. Pursing my lips and raising my eyebrows simultaneously was harder than I imagined and I never quite succeeded in flirting with a female baboon.

Because of my work on "Walking with Cavemen" I finally understood why it's always a little disconcerting looking into the eyes of some of our closest relatives. I couldn't see the whites of baboon eyes because they have brown animal ones. *Homo ergaster*, the creatures on the salt pan, were the first of our ancestors to have white eyeballs. With those it is possible to follow the direction of a stare, essential in building trust and friendship in our highly social species. This book is jam-packed with thought-provoking ideas like that. I never realized just how small some of our ancestors were, or the truly dramatic effects of climatic change on our evolution, or that two, three, perhaps more, species of cavemen shared the same territory at the same time. I'd love to meet them in the flesh and I'm sure after reading this book you'll want to join me.

Introduction

What is it that makes us human? It is a simple but endlessly fascinating question, and the path towards an answer is one of extraordinary adventure and revelation. This book is going to set out on that journey, to explore what makes us special and different from all other creatures on the planet. It is a journey that will cover the globe and reach back through time. It will bring us face to face with the very first human animals that lived on Earth.

Somewhere in our homes each of us can probably find an old photograph album. If we were to open the covers and glance through the photographs, the memories of children, brothers and sisters, cousins, parents – the family – would flood in. Perhaps we would find some faded pictures of our grandparents, great-grandparents or even earlier generations. But that is about as far as most people can go. For a few, there are older images, the occasional glass-plate photograph from the mid-nineteenth century, or a painted family portrait. In the images of our families we see tiny fragments of ourselves staring back. It might be the hook of a grandfather's nose, the crease of a smile, the twinkle of a mother's eyes, something that makes us know that we are part of them. Something that tells each of us, that is *my* family.

Yet in reality, we have only begun to trace our ancestors. Imagine we could go still further back. Ten or twenty generations, and we would be looking at the era of the first circumnavigations of the globe. A sailor among those first shiploads of explorers will have bequeathed parts of his personality and his physique that could be found in some of us alive today, if only we knew exactly who. But why stop there? Fifty generations would take us to the time of the Crusades, a hundred generations to the first stirrings of Ancient

Rome, and yet individuals who lived and died then were also adding to the unique mix of features that define us. If we go back another hundred generations, someone among us is related to Ötzi, the now-famous 'iceman' whose frozen, mummified corpse was discovered in the Italian Alps in 1991, some 5,500 years after he died. Indeed, having isolated DNA from his body and mapped his genetic profile, scientists working on a genetic map of the people of Europe have found a woman living in southern Ireland who is related to him. Something of Ötzi — his physical features, his wits, his creativity — faintly resides in her.

Five hundred generations back, 10,000 years or so ago, life was emerging from the grip of the last ice age. This was the time of 'cavemen', people who dressed in furs, who carved exquisite bone implements and razor-sharp stone blades and who painted the most extraordinary images on their cave walls. The pictures they painted are drawn from their world and their imaginations — their own, long-lasting family album, so to speak. These people were biologically indistinguishable from us. We and these cavemen, the Cro-Magnon, are part of the same human family tree. The skills and traits that they possessed have been handed down to the generations that followed and are found among us today. We are both *Homo sapiens*, carrying the same sense of ancestry and desire to record it for posterity.

But tracing the line of our family into the deep past does not end just yet, for the human story reaches back over lengths of time that are truly awesome in their scale. A thousand generations back would place us still with the cavemen, but at about the time of their earliest known paintings in the caves of southern France. Two thousand generations — 40,000 years — ago, these modern humans had gradually migrated their way out of Africa, through the Middle East, and were beginning to enter Europe, which was still held in the grip of an ice-age climate. However, their human ingenuity and imagination enabled them to survive in the harsh world they were trying to colonize, and to win this land from the people who had long made their home in Europe.

The characteristics that we call 'human' are the product of over 300,000 generations stretching back into our ancestry.

The Neanderthals were our close evolutionary cousins. They dominated Europe for over 200,000 years.

Living in Europe for some 200,000 years had been one of the most successful species of human that ever existed – the Neanderthals.

The Neanderthals mark a very special moment on our journey back into pre-history. They are the people who make us realize that we were not always unique. For so long viewed as mystical creatures from the past, and maligned as brutish ancestors from whom the dark side of our human personality stemmed, the Neanderthals are now known to be another species of human altogether. In effect, they were our human cousins. Indeed, throughout all the generations that precede them there were many other 'human' creatures that shared the world. We tend to think of our ancestry as a continuous line of progression from one extinct 'human' to the next. In fact the dominance of *Homo sapiens* is only very, very recent. The Neanderthals existed in Europe for over 10,000 generations, hunting, cooking, burying their dead, while we were evolving in Africa. For 500 generations, modern humans lived alongside them in Europe, but at the end of that time they had become extinct. Then, for the first time in all of evolution, we were the only human species on the planet.

Yet, just as we can see a family resemblance with our own contemporary cousins, so with Neanderthals and modern humans. If we work further back in our family trees there comes a point where we shared a common inheritance with them – an earlier, pre-human creature gave rise to both us and them. Imagine that we could go back and meet a Neanderthal and look him in the eyes. Such an experience would leave us in little doubt that in this creature was something strongly human. His brain was as large as our own, he would have spoken, he probably would have laughed and cried, although perhaps those responses would have been different to our own. These were people who were self-aware, and conscious of the world around them. Neanderthals had clearly come a long way from our shared earliest ancestors.

So to find the answer to our question – who are we and where did we come from? – we will have to reach back even further through the generations of our early family. Thickset and slightly squatter than we are, the Neanderthals were well adapted to the harsh life they led in icy Europe. In turn, they had inherited characteristics from a creature known as *Homo heidelbergensis*, who appeared in Europe some 10,000 generations before them. *Heidelbergensis* lived for perhaps 300,000 years in Europe, surviving in a vicious world of giant mammals that easily could have killed a man. But *heidelbergensis* were superb hunters who planned their actions, honed their wooden spears, wore down their prey, and butchered their meat with precision. At Boxgrove in southern England, the remains of one of these 'hominids' – for that is the name by which we call all of these pre-human animals – was found amid the debris of what appears to be a stone blade 'factory'. A small mass-production process. we would recognize the 'human' activity there.

If we were to go back and meet these hominids – and much later in this book we shall – the encounter would leave us with a disturbing sense of unease. For in this early human there would be something missing, something that reveals an attitude to life that is distinctly inhuman. No indications have been found that they buried their dead. A defining feature of human society is that we all respond to death in a ritualistic way. But these earlier ancestors did not. It has taken us 20,000 generations to reach back here, but now we are moving into unknown territory. It is becoming harder to see the family resemblance.

Going back even further, we find perhaps the most remarkable hominids of all. *Homo erectus* and its immediate ancestor *Homo ergaster* dominated the planet for over one and a half million years, maybe

Homo heidelbergensis were supremely efficient hunters.

100,000 generations, and it is possible that they died out as recently as just 50,000 years ago in Asia. This was the hominid who first made the great migration out of Africa, striding year on year across the parched plains of the continent, onwards through the Levant and then to the bamboo forests of the Far East. Descendants of *ergaster* were almost certainly the people who entered ice age Europe as *heidelbergensis*. Descendants of *ergaster* were also the people who emerged as modern humans in Africa itself.

Ergaster was tall, smooth-skinned, proportioned in a way that we would instantly recognize as human, but, if we were able to look closer, we would see the head and face of something very different

Homo ergaster was tall, with the first human-like body. It began the great migration of early hominids out of Africa.

indeed. With a low forehead and heavy brow ridge, his face would be that of a wild animal, although one with a glimmer of humanity within. In *ergaster*'s life were the beginnings of very human traits: care for each other, shared child-rearing and a fledgling notion of language. It is a humbling thought that if only we could find the clues, we could track an unbroken line of descent, generation upon countless generation, family after family, from the first *ergaster* to people living and thriving today.

Around two million years ago, Africa was peopled by several different species of ape-man including scavenger *Homo rudolfensis*.

Search further still, and in Africa, around the time that *ergaster* first appeared, we would find a collection of early hominids that co-existed for half a million years. Each was extraordinarily successful at surviving an era of dramatic climate change, by adapting its diet and behaviour. *Homo rudolfensis*, *Paranthropus boisei* and *Homo habilis* were all far more ape-like in appearance than *ergaster*, with fur on their bodies, dark animal eyes, and no hint of language. For *boisei* the future was extinction and oblivion, but for *rudolfensis* and *habilis* (or 'handy man'), the future was more intriguing.

Although we cannot be absolutely sure from which of them we descend, it was certainly from a creature that shared their characteristics, and *habilis* is the most likely to have the accolade of being our direct ancestor. Creatures like *boisei* were specialist feeders, only able to survive with a plentiful supply of the roots that their huge jaws would bite on, while *habilis* had developed the wonderful human trait that we would all recognize: the ability to turn his hand to anything. He could gather fruit, crack nuts and shatter the bones of dead animals to get his food. As the environment changed around him, so he adapted his behaviour to meet the new challenges, and meat became an increasing part of his – and later our – diet. Above all, it is with *habilis* that the first stone

Australopithecus afarensis,
the ape that walked upright.

tools are created, an event that marks the emergence of that crucial human capacity not just to understand the world we live in, but to manipulate it to our advantage.

Where did these ape-like ancestors pick up the fundamental aspects of being human? What set them out on the path that by chance has ended with us? Further back still – three to four million years ago, or 250,000 generations – in the forests of East Africa we discover an animal that is possibly the first to show one of the defining characteristics of our line. Small and chimp-like, with nothing obviously human about their behaviour, these were *Australopithecus afarensis*, the most famous fossil remains of which are from one individual who has become known as Lucy. A glimpse of Lucy would reveal the special characteristic that she bequeathed to her descendants. Lucy walked upright, and that is the clue that tells us she is our ancestor. It is perhaps all we would recognize, but it is not all that binds us to her. In the wrinkle of an ear, the purse of a lip, the furrow of a brow and in a myriad other tiny hidden ways, there are parts of Lucy alive in us all.

In our extraordinary search back through time, we will meet only the family ancestors who are known, for whom fossils have been found and for whom other clues to their lifestyles exist. Probably the traces of many more relatives have been lost over the millennia. We will never know all we would like to know about our origins, but there exists just enough evidence to tell our family history and build up a portrait of the lives of our ancestors. It is a remarkable and epic tale of adventure and ingenuity, driven by the most powerful forces on the planet, and it will unfold in a four-million-year journey from ape to us.

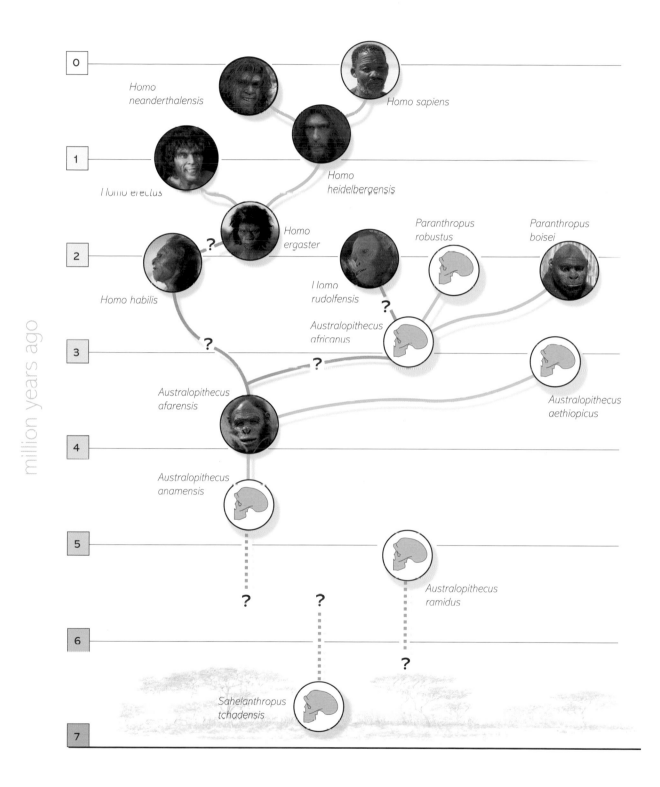

million years ago

0

1

2

3

4

5

6

7

*Homo
neanderthalensis*

Homo sapiens

*Homo
erectus*

*Homo
heidelbergensis*

*Homo
ergaster*

*Paranthropus
robustus*

*Paranthropus
boisei*

Homo habilis

*Homo
rudolfensis*

*Australopithecus
africanus*

*Australopithecus
afarensis*

*Australopithecus
aethiopicus*

*Australopithecus
anamensis*

*Australopithecus
ramidus*

*Sahelanthropus
tchadensis*

A family tree for the hominids showing how they may be related to each other.
The question marks indicate the presence of one or more intermediate species
that are predicted to exist, but for which we have no evidence at present.

3,500,000 YEARS AGO

First Ancestors

The African morning is fresh and cool. The sun has not yet risen, but the sky glows pink on the horizon. The insistent calling of a lone bird is clear and resonant in the still air. As the sky continues to lighten, the dawn chorus begins in earnest, crowding the air with birdsong. In the forest bordering the river, a troop of monkeys descends from the trees to begin the day's foraging.

But these monkeys are not the only primates to have spent the night here. As the sun finally spills over the horizon, a much larger creature rouses himself and climbs down from the messy nest of vegetation in which he slept, his powerful arms supporting his full body weight. He drops gently to the ground and crouches, sniffing the air and scratching through the coarse, dark hair that covers his body. Then, decision made, he rises to his feet and strides off towards the nearby river, pausing only to pluck some ripe berries

(BELOW) Although *afarensis* was adapted for life on the ground, it was also very comfortable up in the trees.

(OPPOSITE) Like all apes, *afarensis* needed to drink regularly, especially as they lived in drier, more open habitats than modern-day apes.

He communicates with… gestures and calls, but he cannot speak.

The *afarensis* looks up startled by a sound. Entirely ape-like in appearance, its only link to modern humans is the fact that it walks on two legs.

that dangle appealingly overhead from the tall bushes. His short, muscular legs allow him to cover the ground swiftly and he is soon hunkered down at the water's edge, drinking his fill. Fully absorbed in gulping down the faintly muddy water, he does not notice a large crocodile slide silently into the river from the sandbank that lies just upstream.

This thirsty individual represents one of the first steps on our journey towards humanity; he belongs to a species known as *Australopithecus afarensis* and he lived three and a half million years ago. His kinship to us is not immediately obvious; in fact, he looks distinctly ape-like. His brain is no larger than that of a chimpanzee and he possesses the short legs and long arms that characterize the great apes of the present day. His face has a pronounced snout, a low forehead and no chin. He feeds on fruit, pods and nuts, and perhaps the odd piece of meat, and while he may use tools to extricate termites from their nests or crack nuts, he does not fashion tools from stone or use them as weapons. He communicates with others of his kind with gestures and calls, but he cannot speak. He possesses none of the intellectual and technological advantages that have allowed modern humans to dominate the planet. But he walks upright, and that is enough to allow him to succeed where other ape-like creatures failed.

The *afarensis* male continues to drink, but a sudden noise startles him and he snaps his head up, his teeth drawn over his lips in a grimace of fear. Hearing the gentle hoots and grunts, he relaxes, realizing it is just the other members of the troop leaving the trees in which they have slept and moving to join him. Under the smooth surface of the water, the crocodile continues to swim closer to the bank, closer to the unsuspecting male, its body weaving through the water sinuously, silently.

The first few heads appear over the tops of the tall grass and the male recognizes the troop's lead female, her infant hanging from her chest, with her adolescent son, who is tagging behind.

On seeing the male, they crouch low to the ground and make a sound midway between a pant and a grunt. They are acknowledging the male's dominance and he responds to their displays of submission with a grunt of his own. As the rest of the troop move down to the river to drink, the male bends his head to take another draught.

His lips have barely touched the surface when the crocodile bursts from the water and grabs the *afarensis* male before he has time to struggle. His head is clamped firmly in the crocodile's jaws as he is pulled underwater into a death roll, the crocodile spinning round and round as the helpless *afarensis* attempts to fight back. But, tough as he is, the *afarensis* is no match for the crocodile, and he cannot escape the powerful, lethal grip of the crocodile's jaws.

On the shore, the other *afarensis* scream with fear and run from the water's edge, leaping back into the trees. The screaming continues despite their move to safety and many animals clutch each other in a tight embrace, seeking comfort in physical contact. From their new vantage point, high above the water, the other members of the troop watch as the crocodile drags the male down for the last time. The churning, foaming water is suddenly quiet, save for a single stream of bubbles that float briefly across the surface.

The dominant male's unfortunate end illustrates, with a stark clarity, that *afarensis* has no special abilities to avoid predation and

Afarensis's small size and lack of sharp teeth meant that it was very vulnerable to attacks by predators such as the crocodile

other dangers. Unlike modern humans, they do not dominate and control their environment, shaping it to suit them. In fact, they are often at a distinct disadvantage since they are small creatures, only 90–120 centimetres (3–4 feet) tall, and they possess no weaponry, such as horns or sharp canine teeth, that can be used in self-defence; nor are they fast enough to outrun any danger that arises. For an *afarensis* individual, survival is a matter of pure chance. They cannot control nature – it controls them.

MEET THE FAMILY

Safe in the trees, the *afarensis* troop begins to calm down, although all are wary of going near the water. Many decide to stay put for the time being, and seek out grooming partners, presenting a shoulder or an arm in the hope that someone will take up their offer. Not only does grooming remove ticks and lice, but the action of combing through another animal's hair calms and soothes both the one that grooms and the one that is groomed. One adult female refuses all such overtures, however, and begins to climb down to the ground, her infant daughter supported on her chest.

The *afarensis* troop retreats to the trees after the attack, the best place for them to avoid danger.

It is the female who first appeared at the waterhole and witnessed the crocodile attack at first hand. Her casual manner and the ease with which she copes with her wriggling infant show that she is well versed in the art of childcare and indeed, at twenty-two years old, she has done this twice before. Her previous offspring are both healthy and still live in the same troop as their mother, although her elder daughter, at almost ten years old, will soon reach maturity and leave to find another *afarensis* troop in which to live.

The infant, although much quieter, is still upset, whimpering in distress, her tiny hands gripping her mother's hairy body. Less than a year old, she is growing rapidly and is constantly hungry. Her mother can barely keep up with her daughter's increasing demand for milk, and spends virtually all her time feeding in order to keep her own energy levels up. She certainly cannot afford to hang around too long in the trees this morning; despite the potential dangers down below, she must start feeding, preferably on the best quality food she can find. This does not present her with too much of a problem since, as the most dominant female in the troop, she can easily displace any of the other females. The males, however, are another matter: they weigh almost twice as much as she does, and they are considerably taller. She does not stand a chance of competing with them, so she must get a head start and go off alone.

The *afarensis* troop is never very cohesive in any case – the twenty animals that make up the female's troop spend most of the day split into small foraging parties, coming together again only in the evening at the trees in which they sleep. This is the most effective way to exploit their woodland home, with its widely dispersed trees and bushes; it not only reduces competition for food between animals, but also helps to cut down on travelling time. If everyone stuck together, they would need to visit many more food trees each day to make sure they all got enough to eat, greatly increasing the distance that would need to be covered. Small parties are much more efficient all round, although predators, like lions, are more likely to attack small groups. However, their climbing abilities help keep them out of danger, and the females in particular never stray too far in the open.

The female does not take too long to find a tree laden with fruit, a particularly good one from her point of view since it is too small to support the weight of the heavier males and she is unlikely to be

(OVERLEAF) *Afarensis*'s strong, muscular arms allowed it to climb trees efficiently.

The female calms her distressed infant. *Afarensis* mothers put a lot of time and effort into caring for their offspring.

disturbed. Climbing up, she scans the canopy to find the branches with the ripest fruit. Settling on a branch, she begins plucking fruits with both hands and shoving them rapidly into her mouth. She sucks out the juice and pulp, wedging the fruit against her teeth, before spitting a soggy wad of skins on to the ground. Grunting in satisfaction, her strong front teeth bite through the thick skin of another fruit, and she grinds the pulp and seeds with her powerful molars. While her

front teeth are rather like a chimpanzee's, albeit narrower, her back teeth are very much larger and extremely well suited to tackling the thick skins and seeds of fruit, as well as the soft juicy flesh. Indeed, *afarensis*'s teeth herald the beginning of a trend for increasing tooth size that will reach its peak, two million years later, in *Paranthropus boisei*, one of the most specialized hominids that ever evolved.

Good climbing abilities were needed to make the most of food resources found high in the trees.

27

How to make a fossil

It may seem as though the evidence on which the story of human evolution is based is rather scanty – a skull here, a knee joint there. With the exception of spectacular fossil finds like Nariokotome Boy (see the feature on pages 124–5), it is true that most finds consist of bits and pieces of bone and teeth. However, considering how fossils are formed, it is remarkable that we have any fossil evidence at all.

Fossilization occurs when once-living matter is replaced by minerals. Although it is commonly thought that fossils are animals that have been literally 'turned to stone', this is not quite true, and most fossils contain much of the original mineral components they possessed in life. For example, many bones retain calcium phosphate, which can be used to provide information about an animal's diet. Fossils can also be more than just bones and teeth; in fact, a fossil can be any remains of life that ends up preserved in rock. Footprints, burrows, even dung, can fossilize. Soft body parts, such as brains, can also fossilize; as sediment fills the brain case of a dead animal it forms a perfect cast of the once living brain (known as an 'endocast').

Fossils can reveal an enormous amount of detail about an animal because mineral replacement takes place at a very fine level; each molecule of living material is individually replaced. This means that fossils can capture extraordinarily subtle details of bones and teeth, such as areas of muscle

attachment on bones and the scratches and pits on teeth caused by chewing food. Scientists can therefore study these features using exactly the same methods and techniques that they use to study material obtained from living specimens.

Not every creature that dies will actually fossilize – it requires a very particular set of circumstances. First, the surrounding sediments must not be too acidic or mineral replacement cannot occur. Rapid burial following death is also useful as this prevents scavengers from eating flesh and bones, and scattering the remains. For these reasons, marine animals or those that live in burrows tend to fossilize well. Areas of volcanic activity often produce large numbers of fossils, as animals are likely to be buried by layers of ash or trapped by molten lava. These sudden catastrophic events also tend to kill large numbers of animals at one time. This increases the likelihood that fossilization will occur by overwhelming the scavenging species and ensuring that at least some bodies are left untouched. Disease epidemics or floods can also have a similar effect.

'Trace' fossils are also likely to be found under volcanic conditions; the Laeotoli footprints (see also the feature on pages 36–7) were created when two *afarensis* individuals left footprints in wet, sandy ground that, by chance, were buried by an ashfall from an erupting volcano. Ancient rivers and lakes are

1 hominid dies

2 body decays and bones are scattered

3 bones buried following volcanic eruption, flash flood etc. and fossilization takes place

4 present day

Fossilization occurs when dead organic matter, like animals and plants, is buried in sediment and minerals replace the bone. Chance plays a large role in which parts of the body are preserved and then found by fossil hunters.

good sources of fossils, as dead bodies are covered by sediment quickly once they come to rest on the bottom and they are less likely to be disturbed once they are buried. Caves preserve bodies well since burial is more likely inside a cave than if bones remain exposed outside – most of the hominid fossils found in South Africa come from cave sites.

Given that volcanic eruptions and epidemics do not happen every day, and that there is no guarantee that an animal will be buried soon after death, it should be apparent that the chances of fossilization occurring are actually very slim, even at the best of times. In some cases, however, the chances of fossilization are virtually nil. Animals living in forest environments rarely fossilize since the conditions are not suitable. Initially, it was thought that dead animals and plants rotted too quickly in these damp, moist habitats – there are many insects, fungi and bacteria that specialize on rotting flesh and an entire carcass can disappear in a matter of days. However, studies of naturally occurring chimpanzee carcasses have shown that bones do not, in fact, decay all that quickly; but they are much less likely to be accidentally buried than in other habitats, and this reduces the chances of fossilization.

Clearly, then, the fossil record does not provide us with a perfect picture of what ancient ecosystems were like. Fossilization is largely a matter of chance, and the chances are better for some kinds of animals than for others. Some species are more likely to fossilize due to their lifestyle and the habitat they occupy, while others possess particular structures that

Almost any trace of life can be preserved in rock to form a fossil. The famous trackway at Laetoli contains the fossilized footprints of two *afarensis* individuals.

increased their likelihood of being preserved. Shells, for example, contain a lot of minerals even before fossilization begins, which makes them hard and more likely to remain intact. Teeth, which are 90 per cent mineral in content, are also likely to fossilize for the same reason. On the other hand, soft-bodied creatures such as jellyfish are much less likely to be represented since their bodies disintegrate before mineral replacement can take place. Another reason that the fossil record is incomplete comes down

to the simple fact that fossils are hard to find: most fossils that exist have not actually been found as yet. For example, it has been estimated that only 3 per cent of all fossil primate species that exist have so far been discovered.

This bias in the fossil record makes it difficult to judge exactly what ancient worlds were like. A fossil could be common either because, in life, the animals themselves were common or because, in death, they were just easily preserved compared to other species. Similarly, fossil hominids are found frequently in or near ancient lakes and river beds, but is this because they actually lived near water, or is it because only those who died near water were fossilized? Are these fossils just easier to find? In order to address these difficulties, a whole new scientific discipline has developed. Known as taphonomy, 'the science of the laws of embedding', its aim is to discover which animals are likely to become fossils, what parts of them are preserved and how these fossils will appear to scientists millions of years later. Taphonomic studies can be used to help correct biases in the fossil record and increase the accuracy with which we can reconstruct past environments and the animals that lived in them.

Afarensis had large, sturdy teeth that developed at a rate similar to modern-day chimpanzees.

Having exhausted the supply of ripe fruits, the female climbs down, heading for some low growing bushes that look promising. Spotting a movement behind her, she turns and catches sight of more members of her troop arriving in the clearing, among them her son. She pants in greeting and he joins her. He has just turned six and the female sees him less often nowadays; for the past year he has been able to feed entirely for himself, and this new-found independence from his mother's milk means he has been able to seek out other *afarensis* for company, particularly the adult males who hold a particular fascination for him.

Estimates of the rate at which *afarensis* youngsters developed are available from analysis of their teeth. The rate at which adult teeth replace the infant milk teeth is distinctive for each primate group. Chimpanzees cut their front teeth – the incisors – at around six years of age, whereas human children usually begin to lose theirs as they approach their seventh birthday, and their adult incisors are not fully grown until they are at least seven and a half. The last teeth to come through, the third molars – the ones we call 'wisdom teeth' – appear in chimps by the time they are eleven, but in humans come through only in the very late teens and, in some cases, may not appear until the mid-twenties. Another difference is that, in chimpanzees, the canine starts to come through before the second molar, while in humans, the canine begins to grow after this tooth appears.

These differences in tooth development reflect a much faster rate of body and brain development in apes compared to humans; an ape's brain is already half its adult size when it is born, whereas a human infant's is only a quarter of its full size. As a result, apes have a much shorter childhood than humans and are ready to breed at an earlier age. Using this information to guide their studies of fossil teeth and jaws, scientists have shown that *afarensis* children were quick developers like apes, reaching adulthood around the age of eleven or so, and living for a maximum of fifty years. Human-like patterns did not appear for another two million years, with the arrival of *Homo ergaster*. The reason will become clear as we continue to follow our ancestors on their journey through time.

THE COMPETITION

Grunting contentedly, mother and son pluck berries from the bushes. The infant, however, is restless and fidgety. Frustrated, her mother dumps her small, squirming body on to the young male, who begins to groom his sister, seemingly content to act as babysitter. The bonds between these two will continue to develop as the baby grows, and she will always be able to look to her older brother for protection against aggression from other members of the troop – something she will need sooner than either of them realize.

Losing all interest in food, the young *afarensis* pair begin some rough and tumble games. Enjoying herself immensely, the infant pulls her lips over her teeth and pants at her brother, making a 'play face'. The peace does not last long, however. A distant screeching carries on the wind, and the mother stops in mid-chew, staring keenly in the direction of the calls. The other *afarensis* feeding nearby also stop, and the males begin to bristle, the hair on their backs and shoulders standing on end. Another scream cuts

Older offspring took a keen interest in new infants, and often acted as babysitters.

across the clearing, closer now, and the infant begins to whimper. Her brother pats her absent-mindedly – he is concentrating hard on the noise, trying to work out where it is coming from. Their mother, tense and agitated, takes the infant back, pulling her close to her chest, and the infant begins to suckle for comfort.

The young male becomes increasingly excited and, spotting a party of adult males on the far side of the clearing, bounds over to them, falling over himself in his eagerness to join them. Two of the highest-ranking males are present in the party, and with the alpha male now dead they are competing for his position. Among

Afarensis males would get rid of tension by performing aggressive displays.

the privileges this brings are mating opportunities. The lead male had fathered most of the infants in the troop, including the female who has fallen asleep, her mother's nipple still in her mouth.

While the cautious contender continues to scan the bushes, the other males scream and chatter wildly to each other, attempting to gauge his reaction, waiting to see if he will lead them off towards the source of the noise. For, unlike this morning, these screams do not herald a predator attack, but the imminent arrival of another *afarensis* troop, intruders attracted by the high-quality foods available in this territory. The threat of violence is real, for both males and females, and the animals are right to show fear. The intruder troop is larger, and has more adult males. They have already beaten one of the *afarensis* males to death and attacked a pregnant female in the last month. The intruders seem intent on eradicating this troop, and taking over their range for themselves.

The other contender for the alpha position, youthful and less experienced, lacks the guarded aggression of the cautious male and finds it hard to keep control. As the males work themselves up into more frenzied bouts of screaming, he grabs a fallen branch and begins flailing it wildly round his head. The females watch, seemingly impressed with this show of strength, while the brash contender whoops in excitement. Bolder now, he swings his new-found weapon at the other male, forcing him to jump for safety. The male screams and charges, but it is too late. He has shown his opponent that he is vulnerable.

Shaken, but in control now, the cautious older male leaves the clearing, followed by the young contender and two of the other adults.

The brash leadership contender flails a stick around his head to increase the impact of his display and intimidate others.

(ABOVE) Climbing up into the trees gives the cautious contender a vantage point from which to scan for potential danger.

(OPPOSITE) Walking upright was a highly efficient way to move between widely spaced food patches, like trees and bushes.

The adolescent male also tags along. He is still excited, and one of the males threatens him; this is no time for juvenile high spirits. The other males are tense and edgy. Chastened by the threat and picking up on their mood, the adolescent falls silent. The cautious contender leads them in single file, at a fast, determined pace. Occasionally, he leaves his position at the head of the patrol, climbing high in the trees to check what lies ahead. Screams are still heard periodically from deep in the woods, and the males pause briefly, before replying with screams of their own. The adolescent male falls behind a little, his legs not strong enough to keep up with the pace. They have travelled at least two kilometres (over a mile) already, but their range is broad, and they have a way to go. There is still no sign of the intruders, but the screams are getting closer.

The pace is stepped up once more, and the adolescent male is beginning to be left behind altogether, when the cautious male suddenly stops, bringing the patrol to an abrupt halt. The calls are directly in front of them. He lets out a terrible scream of his own, then silence falls. The stillness is unnerving and the tension among the males is palpable, each one rigid with concentration. They are close to the boundary of their range, and their leader is wary. The other contender however, still buoyed by his earlier victory, is wild and unruly, flinging himself into trees, screaming hysterically. Unable to stay put any longer, he sets off towards a large clearing just visible through the trees. It is the shortest route to the boundary, but it leaves them completely exposed. Not only is he being foolhardy, he has also made another

Walking tall

The evolution of bipedal walking is probably the most significant of all the features shown by the hominids. Although greatly enlarged brains have been the making of modern humans, this remarkable increase in brain size may never have happened if our earliest ancestors had not evolved to walk upright. However, *afarensis* did not walk exactly as we do. Their anatomy did not commit them irrevocably to life on two feet, but allowed them much greater flexibility in the way they moved around, so they were happy both on the ground and above it.

The biggest differences in *afarensis*'s anatomy, compared to its ape-like ancestors, took place in the lower half of its body. Although its legs were short, more like those of an ape than a human, changes in the structure of the spine, pelvis, thigh-bone and foot meant that *afarensis* could walk completely upright. Unlike the apes, which have a narrow, elongated pelvis reflecting the fact that they use all four limbs to get around, *afarensis*'s is rather squat and shaped more like a bowl. This change in shape was needed so that its pelvis could support the body's internal organs, a job done by the ribs in a four-legged ape. The ilium – the flaring blade of bone on the rear of the pelvis – is also thicker and wider than in apes, increasing the power of the muscles that attach the pelvis to the legs. These muscles, known as the abductors, are crucial for helping to keep the body balanced over the legs, and they

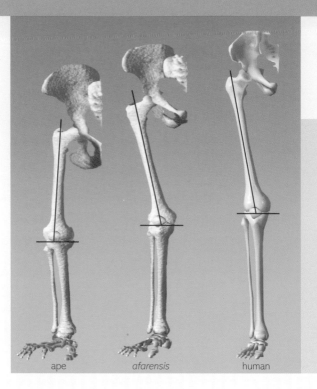

ape   *afarensis*   human

In humans and *afarensis*, the thigh bone slopes in towards the knee forming a distinct angle, known as a valgus angle. This enables the body to balance on one leg while the other is off the ground. Apes have straight thigh bones and are less able to walk fully upright.

stopped *afarensis* from falling over sideways when it lifted up its leg to take a step. The alternating contraction and relaxation of these muscles on each side of the body as *afarensis* lifted each leg in turn meant that its pelvis would have tilted slightly, so that it would have wiggled as it walked, as we do.

Some scientists suggest that while *afarensis* was well designed to stay upright, it could not have walked with the same efficiency as modern humans. They think that *afarensis* would have needed to keep its hips and knees bent slightly when walking, which has been shown to use up more energy than walking with straight hips as we do. It has also been suggested that *afarensis*'s short legs would not have made efficient use of energy, since it would have needed to take more steps to cover the same distance as a long-legged human. However, recent studies on *afarensis*'s

walking abilities by Patricia Kramer of Washington University show that this is not true. Compared to a long-legged modern human, *afarensis* was actually more efficient, not less, and its short legs were not a hindrance to walking efficiently but a positive asset, especially when combined with its wide pelvis. It seems that many scientists assumed that, because we are currently the only surviving bipedal species, our way of walking must be the best way of doing so. The new studies of *afarensis*, in contrast, show us that there is more than just one way to be an efficient biped, and that a wide pelvis and short legs are just as good as, if not better than, our own narrow pelvis and long legs.

As well as having a well-designed pelvis, *afarensis*'s thigh and knee joints are also made for upright walking. Its thigh-bones (femurs) slant inwards from its hips, so that its knees and feet lie

close together. This arrangement is designed to help *afarensis* keep its balance, by bringing its feet directly under its centre of gravity, and it also reduces the amount of energy used when walking. The knee-joint at the end of the thigh is also angled so that it connects properly with the bones of the lower leg, compensating for the slant of the femur. The apes, by contrast, have straight thigh-bones and lack an angled knee-joint. This keeps their feet further apart so that, when they move bipedally, they have to lurch from side to side so that they do not fall over. Apes waddle, rather than wiggle, when they walk upright.

Afarensis's feet have also undergone change, so that they act as platforms that can bear the entire weight of the body, like ours. The Laeotoli footprints, discovered in 1978 by Mary Leakey are the fossilized tracks of two *afarensis* individuals. To some scientists, these show

that *afarensis* had feet much like ours, with a big toe that was lined up with all the others, rather than sticking out to the side like a thumb, in the way that ape toes do. While this is excellent for walking on a flat surface, a foot built like this can no longer grasp, reducing climbing abilities.

Not everyone agrees that *afarensis*'s feet were so human-like, however. Other researchers think that the Laeotoli prints show an ape-like big toe. Fossil evidence from another australopithecine species from South Africa, dated to around the same time as *afarensis* (3.3 million years ago), backs this up. The fossil specimen, nicknamed 'Little Foot', has a thumb-like big toe that could grasp and toes that are long and curved, rather than straight, showing that its feet could still have been used to grasp to at least some degree.

Above the waist, *afarensis* reveals more adaptations for climbing. Its finger bones are curved and longer than ours, and its arms are long, well muscled and incredibly strong. Its upper arms, in particular, were very robust and heavily muscled, so that *afarensis* could haul its body up through the branches, making up for the fact that the feet had lost some of their grasping abilities. However, *afarensis*'s forearms were the same length as humans and much shorter than those of chimpanzees, indicating that it did not use its arms to swing from the branches or hang beneath them to feed. Its skills were in climbing, rather than leaping among the branches, and excellent skills they were too, far outshining even the most athletic bipedal human.

direct challenge to his opponent, who has been making decisions about the route, and he cannot tolerate this.

Their confrontation is brief but loud. Face to face, the younger male realizes how powerful the older male is, and he suddenly lacks the confidence to continue his challenge. What is more, the other males show little sign of supporting him in his efforts. The brash contender drops to the ground, pant-grunting and holding out his hand as a signal of submission. Acknowledging this gesture with a hand on his head, the cautious male sets off in his chosen direction, leading them down towards a fast-flowing river. The rest of the males follow without hesitation, all except the young male, who remains in the clearing. The cautious male turns to check that he is following. Instead of averting his gaze from his victor, as protocol dictates, the brash, young male meets his eye. His baleful glare is not a good sign. This morning's confrontation will not be the last.

Like chimpanzees, *afarensis* males form strong relationships with each other, and spend most of their time together. Females form looser, more casual bonds with males. When females are fertile, temporary courtships between males and females form and they may disappear together for days on end but, as soon as mating is over, the bond breaks down and they go their separate ways. At this stage of evolution, there is no need for exclusive pair bonds, or any division of labour between the sexes. For the moment, males and females are not dependent on each other to cope with life's daily problems. However, the shift to bipedalism is beginning to generate evolutionary pressures that will change this state of

Afarensis groups would split into small foraging parties during the day, often composed of a female and her offspring.

affairs dramatically, the results of which will be felt right down to the present day.

While males and females led independent lives, males were heavily dependent on each other to achieve dominance. They spent a great deal of time grooming, forging bonds and building alliances. An alpha male, in particular, would take trouble to ensure that the other males supported him. He would be well established and have many allies. An alpha male would be in peak physical condition and an impressive combatant. Another male would not stand a chance of defeating him, unless the dominant should suddenly lose power, either through injury or illness, or by losing the support of others. Otherwise, the dominant male would retain this position until he died. The new leader may have to deal with dissent in the ranks, however, this is the least of the his problems at the moment. Across the river, someone is watching them…

The intruder male watches as the patrol moves towards him on the far bank. Sensing his group mates pushing up behind him, he threatens them with a soft coughing bark and they move back. He shifts position for a better look, and the branches around him shake. Back on the other side of the river, the movement catches the dominant male's eye. Realizing he has been spotted, the intruder male emerges from the bush, staring at the dominant, challenging him. The males in the patrol begin to sway from side to side, agitated, and once again their hair begins to stand on end. Behind the intruder, there is further movement as the remaining members of his party emerge from the bushes, and the two groups face off across the water.

Grooming was an essential part of *afarensis*'s daily life, helping to form bonds, as well as keep clean and lice-free.

The *afarensis* patrol faces off the intruders on the opposite river bank.

The skirmish erupts in a frenzy of screams and hoots. The males in the patrol become wildly aggressive, jumping from the trees to the ground and climbing back again, tearing off branches and hurling them across the river. The intruders respond in kind, heaving rocks, many of which fall short of their target, sending fountains of water into the air, adding to the chaos. The brash contender, still harbouring aggression and resentment over his failed dominance bid, releases all his pent-up hostility in a magnificent threat display, leaping around on a low-hanging branch jutting out over the water. Some of the males on the other side begin to display in similar fashion, but neither party seems to want to take things further. The sides are too evenly matched to risk real violence; their displays are merely an effort to reinforce the boundaries between their ranges.

Gradually, the young contender's display begins to wind down. He leaps on to the bank and lands close to the adolescent male, who greets him with a barrage of frantic hoots and barks. Listening to their frenzied screams, it is hard to see these creatures as anything other than apes. But as the encounter comes to an end, they do something that no ape has ever done nor ever will: they stand upright and they walk away on two legs.

Our link to *afarensis* immediately becomes clear with this one simple action; it moves in a way that is unique to the family of hominids to which we, as modern humans, belong. None of our other primate cousins moves like this, and it brings with it advantages that will shape human evolution for millions of years to come. But how did such a strange trait come about? Why exactly did evolution suddenly favour apes who stood on their own two feet? To find out, we need to leave *afarensis* and travel further back in time: another four million years.

Although *afarensis* can move efficiently on two feet, they were not very speedy and could not run like modern humans.

Female *afarensis* were especially vulnerable to predator attack and probably never moved very far from the safety of the trees.

BACK TO THE FUTURE

The green-filtered light of the forest casts a ghostly glow on the thick, twisting ropes of lianas that snake between the trees. Birds dart swiftly among the gaps in the canopy, chasing insects on the wing, silent but for the noise of their wings as they whip through the air. Giant spider webs, white and gauzy, hang between the branches like ruined sails. The air is damp and humid, the thick beds of leaf litter giving off a strong, earthy smell. The forest is alive with rustlings in the tree tops and strange howling calls, but it is impossible to see the creatures that are making them. Clearly, we are no longer in the world of *afarensis* – but we have travelled only in time, not space. We are still in Africa, but four million years before *afarensis* existed. At this point in time, seven million years ago, an unbroken sea of primary rainforest stretches across Africa, extending for thousands of kilometres in all directions. This type of forest covers many other parts of the world too, since the planet is warmer than it is today and capable of supporting this more luxuriant vegetation.

This is a world in three dimensions – the creatures that live here are as happy 100 metres (300 feet) up in the air as they are on the ground – happier perhaps, since many unseen dangers lurk on the forest floor. These are animals that can move as easily up and down as they can from left to right. Many of the animals that inhabit this forest are very like the monkeys and apes that we see today. But there is also a creature here that no human has ever seen.

Somewhere in this ancient forest lived an ape species for which there is not a trace of evidence. We do not have a single fossil to tell us anything about how it looked or lived. But we know that it existed. How can we be so sure? Because genetic evidence shows that the chimpanzee line split off from the hominids somewhere between five and seven million years ago, which means that the species that gave rise to all of us, chimpanzees, *afarensis* and the rest – our common ancestor – must have lived in this immense forest.

This animal was not bipedal, but it may have been a knuckle-walker, like modern-day apes, supporting its upper body on the backs of its hands. Resting on the knuckles holds the body semi-erect when the animal is walking on the ground, whereas for a truly four-footed animal, the body is horizontal. Since evolution works by tinkering with the body structures that already exist, rather than evolving new ones completely from scratch, an ancestor that was already half-upright would be the simplest path for evolution to take. An alternative scenario is that the ancestral species was a small 'brachiator', an animal that used its arms to swing through the trees, like modern-day gibbons. Gibbons always walk on two feet on the rare occasions that they come to the ground, their long arms held above their head in a fashion that seems rather comical to our eyes; but such a strategy may have helped *afarensis*'s ancestor to make the switch from the trees to the ground.

Afarensis may have evolved its upright posture from an animal that walked on its knuckles, like modern-day apes.

Raymond Dart and the Taung child

Although the East African species of *afarensis* is one of the earliest known hominids, it was not the first to be discovered. The first australopithecine was found in South Africa, over seventy-five years ago, by Raymond Dart.

Dart was Australian by birth and studied medicine at the University of Sydney, but he eventually made his home in South Africa, taking up the post of Professor of Anatomy at the University of the Witswatersrand in Johannesburg. He arrived at the beginning of 1923 and was soon inspiring students with his

Raymond Dart with his famous discovery, the Taung child, officially known as *Australopithecus africanus*.

lectures – although by all accounts his students learned considerably more about Dart himself than they did about anatomy. Since the department was poorly supplied with skeletons, Dart offered small prizes to any student who could provide him with interesting specimens. One student produced an extremely impressive fossil baboon skull that she had borrowed from a friend. Dart was intrigued by the find and discovered that it had come from a lime works around the tiny village of Taung, near the Kalahari Desert. Dart contacted the manager of the lime works and arranged to have any fossils packed in boxes and sent to him.

Two enormously heavy boxes duly arrived on a summer's day in 1924. At first Dart was disappointed with his 'treasure', as the first box contained little more than some fossil eggshells. But in the second crate, Dart made a truly historic discovery. There on top of the rubble was an endocast – the fossilized remains of a brain. Dart immediately saw that it was a primate, but it was like no monkey or ape endocast he had ever seen. Sorting through further, Dart found a skull, still encased in rock (or 'breccia' as its known) into which, remarkably, the endocast fit perfectly.

Using a hammer, a chisel and some sharpened knitting needles, Dart spent months chipping away at the rock surrounding the fossil. Gradually, the most delightful fossil emerged: it had a small, delicate face, an intact lower jaw

and, although the bones of the skull were missing, their shape and size could be gauged from the endocast. All the teeth were present, and showed that the creature was not fully grown, but a juvenile at the time it died. Dart estimated it was around six years of age, although modern estimates suggest it was nearer two to three years old. The near vertical face and small teeth led Dart to the conclusion that this was not an ape, but something far more human. This suspicion was confirmed when he found pieces of bone attached to the endocast that made up the edge of the foramen magnum, the 'great hole' through which the spinal cord leaves the brain. Unlike an ape's, the tiny creature's foramen was positioned underneath the skull, pointing downwards. This meant that the head had been balanced directly on top of the spine. Dart knew of only one other primate that showed this feature – modern humans – and they did so because they walked on two legs. Stunned, Dart realized that his Taung child had also walked upright.

By 1925, Dart was convinced he had found the 'missing link' and wrote up his findings for the eminent British journal, *Nature*, naming the fossil *Australopithecus africanus* – the southern ape of Africa.

Initially, Dart's paper was met with enthusiasm. Even General Jan Smuts, the South African Prime Minister, sent a message of congratulation. But not everyone was impressed. The British scientific establishment, in particular,

The exquisite Taung child fossil. The face and jaws are beautifully preserved and the endocast of the brain can be seen fitting snugly into the skull.

on the skull, he abandoned fossil work, and suffered a nervous breakdown. His precious child was left in a box on a colleague's desk, abandoned and forgotten.

Luckily for Dart and the Taung child, there was someone who believed in them both – Robert Broom. Like Dart, Broom was a palaeontologist-cum-doctor who had made South Africa his adopted home. He also had strong, eccentric views but, unlike Dart, he was not one to lose confidence in his own opinion. He did not trust the opinion of others either, and so arranged to see the Taung skull for himself. Upon examining the skull, Broom was fully convinced that Dart was correct and everyone else was wrong. Determined to set the record straight, Broom wrote to a leading Oxford academic and convinced him that Dart's interpretation was accurate.

Later, Broom was also able to continue fossil hunting himself. By the 1930s, Broom had found an adult skull of *africanus* (known as 'Mrs Ples'). By the 1950s, other parts of the skeleton had been discovered as well, including parts of the femur and pelvis, proving beyond a shadow of a doubt that *africanus* was a bipedal hominid. Dating techniques estimated that *africanus* lived between 2.8 and 2.3 million years ago, while studies of its anatomy showed that it shared many features of its skull with *Homo*, leading some scientists to suggest that it lay close to the ancestry of species such as *Homo habilis*. Far from being a juvenile ape, *africanus* was a fully paid-up member of the hominid family. Raymond Dart had been right all along.

was having none of it. Just a week later, *Nature* was publishing articles criticizing Dart's interpretation (all of which, it should be noted, were written by people who had never actually seen the original fossil). Arthur Keith, from the Royal College of Surgeons, was one of the most vocal critics. Keith could not accept the Taung child as the missing link because it had a small ape-like brain but a very human-like face, jaws and teeth. For him, this was entirely the wrong way round. Keith was convinced that large

brains had appeared at a very early stage of human evolution, long before any other changes had taken place. He put all his faith in Piltdown Man as the missing link – a big mistake on his part (see the feature on pages 162–3).

Keith and his followers rejected the Taung fossil and questioned Dart's anatomical skills – how could he have mistaken a young ape for a human ancestor? Dart never really recovered from this humiliating public assault. Giving up his plans to publish a book

Although the ground beneath our feet appears stable and solid, appearances are deceptive. The Earth is dynamic and constantly changing.

Whichever of these is true – something we may never know for sure – it still does not answer the question of why these changes happened in the first place. What caused the shift to a two-legged life on the ground? The answer lies not in the African rainforest, but half a world away, with a series of events that altered this planet for ever.

Although the ground beneath our feet appears stable and solid, appearances are deceptive. The Earth is dynamic and constantly changing. Beneath the surface, our planet has a boiling, churning centre of molten rock, known as magma. The thin crust, on which we live, is also less stable than we imagine. It is not continuous, but forms a dozen or so large plates, which ride on top of the magma and move against each other constantly. Throughout the Earth's vast history, these continental plates have joined up and separated, buckling and contorting the huge land masses that lie on top of them, altering the planet's climate and having dramatic effects on its plants and animals.

In a process beginning over forty million years ago, these slow movements of the continental plates gradually shunted India – which at the time was a massive floating island – into the main body of the Asian continent. This clash of land masses pushed up a vast kink of rock, forming the largest range of mountains on earth: the Himalayas. At 8 kilometres (5 miles) high and over 3,000 kilometres (2,000 miles) long, the emergence of this enormous range had an extraordinary effect on the Earth's atmosphere. Moist air drawn from the Indian Ocean was no longer able to get past the vast barrier formed by the Himalayas. Instead, the clouds were forced to drop their load over India, causing some of the heaviest rainstorms the world had ever seen: today we call them the monsoons. These immense rainstorms meant that the air that continued westwards lacked moisture. As it passed over the Middle East and on to East Africa, it started to have a drying effect. Although the story is complicated, experts think that, around six to seven million years ago, a threshold was reached when the climate changed sufficiently to cause a shift in the type of vegetation that could survive in these areas. The moist forests that once flourished in East Africa gradually began to dry up and die out.

Climatic change converted the vast African rainforest into the mosaic of woods and bushland in which *afarensis* thrived.

But the formation of the Himalayas and the monsoons was not the only event that helped to reshape the African continent. Around fifteen million years ago, the margin of the continental plate that lay below East Africa began 'doming', with huge uplifts of lava being pushed up from the gap between the plates and creating uplifts 1,000 metres (over 30,000 feet) in height. Weakened by the separating plates, the continental rock gradually began collapsing in a long, vertical fault, several thousand kilometres long and up to three kilometres (nearly two miles) deep. Today, we know this as the Great Rift Valley. The effect of this huge tear in the Earth's surface was to throw the eastern side of the continent into rain shadow. This deprived it of moisture and further exaggerated the drying effect induced by the monsoons in Asia.

It is possible that one of the reasons *afarensis* walked on two legs was to allow it to see over the tall grasses that formed much of its habitat.

To the west of Rift Valley, there was little or no change; the rainforests continued to receive enough moisture to survive, and the creatures that lived in them continued on the evolutionary path that led to the modern-day chimpanzees and gorillas. But on the eastern side of the Rift Valley, it was a different story as huge swathes of forest died back, leaving a mosaic of swamps, bushy woodlands and open grasslands. Forest could only occur along the margins of rivers where there was still sufficient water to support large trees. For the creatures caught in this great transformation, the pressures to adapt were enormous; the specializations that made each species successful in a dense forest environment no longer worked in a more open, patchy habitat. Vast changes in anatomy and behaviour were needed to exploit this new world effectively. In all, it took four million years to change a forest-living ape into one that could cope with life in the woodlands of the new East Africa. It was a new kind of ape altogether – an upright ape, with strong legs designed for walking on the ground – an ape called *afarensis*.

So why exactly did *afarensis* walk upright? Why did this single adaptation make it so successful? Some scientists have suggested that the advantage of standing upright is related to the way that it allowed *afarensis* to develop new behaviours. For example, with its hands no longer needed for walking, it would have been able to carry food or dependent young more efficiently. Similarly, standing on two legs increased *afarensis*'s height, allowing it to peer over tall grasses in order to spot potential dangers. More recently, though, scientists have realized that walking on two legs would have benefited *afarensis* directly in terms of allowing it to cope with the environmental demands of its new habitat.

In all, it took four million years to change a forest-living ape into one that could cope with life in the woodlands

49

Ancestors before *afarensis*

When *Australopithecus afarensis* was first discovered by Donald Johanson, back in 1974, it was the oldest fossil hominid that had ever been found. Since then, however, other fossil finds have been challenging *afarensis* for that title.

One contender for the earliest fossil hominid is *Ardipithecus ramidus.* Fossils of this species were found in Ethiopia during the early 1990s, including a number of teeth, skull and arm bones, calculated to be approximately 4.4 million years old. *Ardipithecus* is much more ape-like than *Australopithecus afarensis,* with thin tooth enamel, very large canine teeth and an elbow that can be 'locked' into position to aid tree-climbing. These features have led some researchers to suggest that *Ardipithecus* was not just ape-like, but actually was an ape. However, other scientists insist that there are features of *Ardipithecus*'s anatomy that are distinctly hominid. One key feature is the lack of a 'honing facet' on the lower pre-molar tooth (the next tooth along from the canine). In apes, this tooth is ground against the canine in the upper jaw and helps keep it sharp. All known ape species have this feature, but no hominid grinds its teeth in this way. More intriguingly, a small fragment of the skull of *Ardipithecus* appears to show that the foramen magnum is positioned underneath, as in hominids (although much further forwards than in any other species), rather than towards the back like the quadrupedal apes,

suggesting that *Ardipithecus* walked on two legs. However, this is circumstantial, rather than conclusive, evidence, and a better knowledge of *Ardipithecus*'s legs and pelvis are needed to confirm that it was indeed bipedal.

Ardipithecus ramidus lost its record as the oldest potential hominid in 2001 to *Ardipithecus ramidus kadabba,* another Ethiopian find, estimated to have lived around 5.8 to 5.6 million years ago – very close to the time when the ape and hominid lines diverged from their common ancestor. At present, there are eleven fossil specimens from at least five different individuals, including a partial jaw with teeth, hand, foot and arm bones and a collarbone. The fossils are very similar to those of *Ardipithecus ramidus,* especially the teeth, and so the new find is considered to be a sub-species of *ramidus,* rather than an entirely new species. However, although the teeth are similar, *kadabba*'s teeth are much more ape-like than the younger *ramidus* fossils, as might be expected given that it lies closer to the root of the ape and human lines.

Both *ramidus* and *kadabba* are estimated to have been the size of a chimpanzee, standing 122 centimetres (4 feet) tall. They also had ape-like brain and limb proportions. However, a toe-bone from *kadabba* indicates that it may not have been ape-like when it came to moving around. The shape of this bone indicates that the animal probably moved by pushing off with its toes while

Donald Johanson discovered Lucy otherwise known as *Australopithecus afarensis* in 1974, but since then even older hominid fossils have been found.

keeping its heel above the ground, a feature characteristic of bipedal walking and one found in both *afarensis* and modern humans.

Again, this evidence is not entirely convincing, and further proof from the leg bones is needed in order to make a solid case for bipedalism, and to substantiate the claim that *Ardipithecus* should be considered as a hominid. Indeed, some researchers consider this evidence so flimsy that they view *kadabba* as an extinct ape species that played no part in subsequent human evolution. Instead, they argue that an even older fossil, *Orrorin tegenensis* (known as Millennium Man since it was announced in the year 2000), is the real link between the apes and the later hominids. Somewhat surprisingly, however, given the criticisms of *Ardipithecus,* it turns out that there is no firm evidence to prove that this species was a hominid either, although the researchers who found these fossils claim that the femur of *Orrorin* shows it was bipedal, and what is more was actually a better biped than *afarensis.*

The newly discovered Toumaï skull complicates matters even further (see the feature on pages 56–7) and this state of affairs means that it is very hard to decide at present which species, if any, is actually a hominid. Hopefully, as more details of these species emerge, we will have a better idea if we have found our very earliest ancestor, or just a side-branch of the human family.

While controversy rages about *Ardipithecus* and the like, there is another early species that is undoubtedly a hominid and undoubtedly bipedal. This species is known as *Australopithecus anamensis* and has been dated to four to four and a half million years old. As with *Ardipithecus,* the fossil evidence is fragmentary, consisting of the bottom half of the humerus (the upper arm bone), an almost complete tibia (the larger of the two lower leg bones), parts of the skull and jaws, and isolated teeth. The tibia provides the crucial evidence that *anamensis* was bipedal. There are

A reconstruction of *Australopithecus anamensis.* Since the remains of this species are fragmentary, a lot of imagination had to go into making this for an exhibition, as well as anatomical knowledge.

several features of the knee-joint, in particular, that show that this creature shifted its weight from one leg to the other when it was moving, something which is unquestionably associated with human-like bipedalism. Indeed, both the tibia and the humerus (in particular, the elbow region) are very human-like – much more so than *afarensis.* Aspects of the skull and teeth, on the other hand, are very similar to those of *afarensis,* with thick tooth enamel and large, broad molars.

This presents a rather intriguing, somewhat paradoxical, picture. *Anamensis* is very primitive in terms of its jaws and teeth, but very human-like

in terms of its knee and elbow joints. This obviously complicates the picture we have of human evolution since, in *anamensis,* we have a fossil that is older than *afarensis,* yet it shows advanced bipedal characteristics very like those of the more recently evolved *Homo* species. This could mean that *anamensis* is not related to *afarensis,* but represents another hominid line entirely, indicating that the hominid family tree was already quite bushy four million years ago, with more than one species present. As with *Ardipithecus,* we need more detailed evidence, and many more fossils, before we can be sure of how all these species fit together, and which, if any, are our direct ancestors.

the shift to bipedalism made by *afarensis* opens up a wealth of opportunities for the human line

One theory suggests that standing upright allowed *afarensis* to keep its body temperature at an acceptable level when foraging out in the open, especially during the hot midday period. An upright body presents only the top of the head and the shoulders to the full glare of the sun, rather than the whole back, helping to keep a body cool and preventing dangerous overheating. However, the fact that *afarensis* lived in a quite wooded habitat, with lots of shade, suggests that overheating may not have been such a problem for them. Instead, the most likely explanation is that the short-legged bipedalism shown by *afarensis* is simply the most efficient and effective means of moving between widely dispersed food resources.

Using mathematical models to reconstruct *afarensis*'s way of moving, scientists have shown that a female *afarensis* would have used less energy per step compared to a knuckle-walker or a modern human woman, and would have been more energy-efficient overall as a result. The increase in efficiency is not huge: by walking on two legs, *afarensis* saves only around 300 grams of fat each year – the equivalent of a single packet of biscuits – but the difference is crucial. With less energy spent on moving around, *afarensis* could put more energy into the activity that drives the whole of evolution: reproduction. The energy savings made by *afarensis* allowed it to recover faster after the birth of an infant, to provide better care and nourishment for each offspring, and to start reproducing at a younger age. In short, by standing up, an *afarensis* individual was able to produce more children in its lifetime and, as far as evolution is concerned, that is what life is all about.

The success of *afarensis* stems from its unique blend of ape and human characteristics. But it would be a serious mistake to see *afarensis* as some sort of compromise between the two. It is not an inferior kind of human, nor a superior type of ape, but a highly

successful species in its own right, with a unique and effective way of getting around. And the shift to bipedalism made by *afarensis* opens up a wealth of opportunities for the human line, far beyond those that originally made walking on two feet a success; *afarensis*'s small steps are already paving the way for the giant leaps of mankind.

During the middle of the day, when it was too hot to forage, the *afarensis* troop would take a break to rest and groom each other.

THE SEXUAL IMPERATIVE

Back in the clearing, the females have been feeding ever since the departure of the males. So intent are they on eating their fill that it seems no time at all before a hooting from beyond the clearing heralds the males' return. The adolescent male, now more boisterous than ever following his sojourn in the adult world, runs to his mother and pulls his sister from her arms. He begins to chase her around the clearing, working off the rest of his nervous energy, glad to be back among his family. His mother, meanwhile, greets the new lead male, and he offers his shoulder for grooming. Smacking her lips, the female settles down beside him and is soon engrossed in her efforts – until, that is, her son gets too rough with his infant sister, who begins to scream in fear. Breaking off from grooming, the female is forced to rescue her youngest offspring, threatening her over-excited son as she does so. With her daughter hanging from her side, the female retreats behind some bushes where, shielded from the rest of the group, she attempts to calm the infant.

Alarmed, the female spins round and, surprised to find herself alone with him, she barks in fear.

Only the brash contender notices her leave and, surreptitiously checking on the rest of the troop, he follows her. As he leaves, the calls of the rival troop can be heard once again; this morning's boundary dispute did not decide things after all. The dominant male, hair on end, runs from the clearing, the adolescent male and the rest of the adult males close behind. The young contender watches them pass from his vantage point behind the trees, but he does not join them. Instead, his gaze returns to the female who, oblivious to his presence, plays with and grooms her daughter.

The male approaches the pair. His intent is sexual, although the female is not yet ready to mate again. She is still breast-feeding and this inhibits the release of eggs from her ovaries, so for the moment she is infertile. However, if the young contender can engage her in grooming now, forming a bond between them, she may choose to mate with him when the time is right. The female is still unaware of the male's presence, however, and is lazily picking berries, watching as her infant discovers the joy of playing with sticks. The male reaches out and touches her on the shoulder as a prelude to grooming. Alarmed, the female spins round and, surprised to find herself alone with him, she barks in fear.

The male, in his turn, is unsettled by the female's reaction. Still tense from this morning's frustrating interactions with his

Male *afarensis* were much bigger and stronger than females, and probably didn't hesitate to use aggression to get what they wanted.

The earliest ancestor of all?

For many of the fossil hunters interested in human evolution, a major goal has been to find the 'missing link': the species that represents the last common ancestor between apes and humans, one that gives us an insight into the very deepest roots of humanity. In July 2002, with great fanfare, a team lead by Michel Brunet of the Université de Poitiers, France, announced the discovery of such a link: the Toumaï skull, a fossil with both ape and hominid characteristics and one that lies closer to the origins of the hominid line than any other fossil yet discovered. Brunet and his colleagues claim that Toumaï, at an estimated six to seven million years old, is the oldest hominid ever discovered, pushing back the date at which the ape and human lines split from each other by at least a million years. As we shall see, however, not everyone is convinced that this is the case.

One very interesting and intriguing feature of Toumaï is that it was found not in East Africa, where the majority of hominid fossils have been found, but over 2,500 kilometres (1,550 miles) away, in Chad, Central Africa, indicating that the early hominids had a much wider geographical range than anyone had anticipated. This means that some changes may be needed to the 'East Side Story' of human evolution, which suggests that hominids evolved only in East Africa, in response to the particular set of environmental conditions that existed there following the creation of

The beautifully preserved Toumaï skull. Is it a hominid ancestor or an ancient ape?

the Rift Valley. The discovery of Toumaï (which means 'hope of life' in the local Goran language) implies that similar environmental pressures leading to the evolution of the hominid line were present in other areas too. While an earlier discovery in 1995, named *Australopithecus bahrelghazali,* in the same region of Chad had already revealed that the early hominids had moved beyond East Africa by around three and a half million years ago, the great age of the Toumaï skull suggests that hominids could either have evolved outside East Africa altogether or that they evolved in more than one place at the same time.

In addition to the almost complete skull of Toumaï, two lower jaw fragments and three isolated teeth have also been discovered. All these fossils have been assigned to a completely new species,

Sahelanthropus tchadensis, due to its unique mixture of ape and hominid features. Like the hominids, it has small canine teeth and it lacks a 'honing facet' on its lower pre-molar tooth, a key feature distinguishing apes from hominids. As well as these differences in the teeth, *Sahelanthropus* also has a less protruding face than an ape, combined with a heavy and continuous brow-ridge of a kind that is more characteristic of the genus *Homo* than of the great apes.

This heavy visor-like brow-ridge has led Brunet and his colleagues to suggest that Toumaï was a male. However, without bones from the rest of the body, it is not possible to state this with absolute certainty. This is crucial since, if Toumaï turns out to be a female, then it may not be a hominid after all, since female apes also have heavy brow-ridges in combination with small canines and a small face. If Toumaï is actually female, then *Sahelanthropus* is better characterized as an ancient form of ape, rather than a very early hominid. Indeed, Toumaï has an ape-size brain of around 280–320 cubic centimetres (45–51 cubic inches) and there are a number of other features of the skull-bones that are more similar to those of apes than to the other hominid species. Even if this proved to be the case, however, *Sahelanthropus* would still be an enormously important species since, at long last, we would know in some detail what the last common ancestor (or something very like it) of apes and humans looked like.

Another controversial feature of Toumaï is the position of the foramen magnum (the hole in the base of the skull through which the spinal cord passes). As the base of the skull has been distorted during fossilization, it is quite difficult to work out exactly how this must have looked when the creature was alive, but Brunet and his colleagues suggest that the foramen was positioned forwards on the skull so that the head balanced on top of the spine and, therefore, that *Sahelanthropus* could have been bipedal. However, other scientists think that the foramen was probably positioned towards the back of the skull, as it is in chimpanzees, which would mean that *Sahelanthropus* moved on four legs rather than two.

The dating of the skull also needs to be confirmed more precisely. At present, the fossils have been dated by looking at the other fossil animals found with the skull, and comparing these to other fossil sites where exact dates are known.

Michel Brunet compares *Sahelanthropus* with the skull of a modern chimpanzee. The large brow-ridge and small jawbones of *Sahelanthropus* differ substantially from those of male apes, and are considered to be distinctive hominid features.

While this technique can be very accurate (see feature on pages 108–9) the studies of the other fossil animals have not been fully completed and so, at this stage, the age of the fossil needs to be treated cautiously.

As well as giving clues about the age of *Sahelanthropus,* these other fossil animals provide information about the kind of habitat in which it lived. So far, more than 700 specimens have been found, including fish, crocodiles and rodents, suggesting that *Sahelanthropus* lived in an area with a diverse range of habitats, including wet forest and lakes.

If *Sahelanthropus*'s status as the oldest and most primitive hominid so far discovered is confirmed, it raises all sorts of fascinating questions about the role it played in subsequent human evolution. Brunet and his team suggest that *Sahelanthropus* could be a 'sister group' to more recent species, rather than a direct ancestor, emphasizing that, even at this very early stage, the human evolutionary tree had a number of side-branches. However, as Brunet points out, much more detailed analyses and more fossils are needed before we can make any reliable suggestions of patterns of relatedness between these ancient hominids. No doubt there will be plenty more surprises in store.

(PREVIOUS PAGE) The female *afarensis* is powerless to stop a potentially infanticidal attack on her offspring.

attacking and killing youngsters can help increase a male's reproductive success

cautious opponent, he seizes her roughly and begins to grapple with her, his intention merely to force the female to groom, but she resists. His body forms a barrier between the mother and her infant, and the infant begins to whimper. Hearing her baby cry, the female tries to push past the male, her arms flailing. Misconstruing her action as an attack, the male snarls and launches himself at her, landing a punishing blow on her back. What was intended as a harmless exercise in bridge-building has mutated into an all-out fight.

The other adult males, still close enough to hear the female's screams, rush back, her son leading the way. He hurtles into the clearing to find his mother facing off against the young male. Moving between them, he tries to defend her. The male moves forward menacingly, but the arrival of the other males stops him, and he backs off. The female immediately scoops her infant from the ground, once again having to comfort her terrified offspring. But the aggressive male has not finished yet.

Facing the other males, he draws his lips over his teeth in a grimace, half-fear, half-threat. Unsure what he is up to, the other males watch him closely. Suddenly, before anyone has time to act, he leaps at the female, knocking her to the ground, snatching the infant from her and bounding off into the undergrowth. In his highly charged, testosterone-fuelled state, the male is about to attempt the most shocking of all ape behaviours: infanticide.

Studies of modern apes have shown that attacking and killing youngsters can help increase a male's reproductive success in two ways. First, it increases the male's chance of mating by bringing the mother back to a fertile state, by removing the inhibitory effect that suckling has on egg production. Second, by killing another male's offspring, he reduces their reproductive success relative to his own, so that more of his genes are passed on to the next generation.

Australopithecus afarensis

Who discovered *afarensis*?

The most famous *afarensis* specimen – and possibly the most famous fossil hominid ever – is Lucy (her 'official' name is A.L.288), who was found by Donald Johanson and Tom Grey at Hadar, Ethiopia, in 1974. The name *afarensis* was chosen as the species name because the Hadar site is located in a region known as the Afar triangle. Her nickname was given to her in honour of the Beatles song 'Lucy in the Sky with Diamonds', which was playing in their field camp on the night they celebrated their amazing discovery.

When did *afarensis* live?

The Lucy fossil has been dated to 3.2 million years ago. Another remarkable find by Johanson – the First Family (A.L. 333), which are the remains of at least thirteen individuals of all ages all found in the same place – are slightly older and dated to around 3.4 million years ago. *Afarensis* fossils have also been found at the Ethiopian sites of Belohedelie (a frontal skull bone), Maka (the upper end of a forearm) and Fejej (some isolated teeth). These are estimated to be older than the Hadar fossils: the Belohedelie and Maka finds are dated to between 3.46 and 3.7 million years old, while the Fejej teeth may be as much as four million years old. *Afarensis* fossils have also been discovered in Laeotoli, Tanzania, and range in age from 3.46 to 3.7 million years old. Laeotoli is most famous as the 'footprint site' where, in 1978, Mary Leakey discovered a trackway containing the fossilized prints of two *afarensis* individuals.

Where did *afarensis* live?

To date, Ethiopia and Tanzania are the only countries in which *afarensis* has been found. Nevertheless, the large distance between these two countries shows that the species was very widespread across East Africa in its time.

What would *afarensis* have looked like?

Approximately 40 per cent of Lucy's skeleton was found, which at the time made her the most complete fossil hominid in existence. The structure of her pelvis, femur (thigh-bone) and tibia (lower leg bone) showed that she was, without doubt, bipedal. However, in most other respects, *afarensis* was a very ape-like species. Lucy was estimated to have been around 107 centimetres tall (3 feet 6 inches) – rather small for an *afarensis* – and weighing about 28 kilograms (62 pounds). The size and stride patterns of the Laeotoli footprints indicate that the individuals that made them were probably about 140 centimetres (4 feet 8 inches) and 120 centimetres (4 feet) tall. Males are thought to have been twice the size of females but were still no taller than around 160 centimetres (just over 5 feet). Despite its upright stance, *afarensis* was a very short animal indeed. The large size difference between the sexes suggests that males had to compete strongly for mating rights within

Male *Australopithecus afarensis*.

a group, rather like modern-day chimpanzees. Females may also have been at risk from infanticidal attacks by males, and so were likely to have mated with as many males as possible in order to confuse paternity so that males had no idea who really was the father of a female's offspring.

How would *afarensis* have lived?

Studies of *afarensis*'s teeth suggest that they were fruit eaters, but the large size of their molar teeth show that they were also capable of eating quite tough foods, such as acacia pods or underground corms. Although adept at walking upright, they were also very good at climbing, using their arms to lever them up through the branches. They probably lived in groups of around twenty to thirty animals that split up into smaller parties to forage.

As the male tears through the undergrowth, the infant's mother and the other males give chase, desperate to save the infant, heedless of the thorns that catch on their hair and skin. Their screams carry to the brash contender, who is losing ground as they move into the dense woodland that runs along the river. Confronted by a tangle of thorns that he cannot penetrate, the male is forced to turn and confront his pursuers. Dropping the infant, he displays at them with ferocious snarls, while the infant, bruised, shaken but thankfully alive, crawls into the undergrowth to safety. The male steps up his display, but it is the new leader who attacks first, throwing himself at the young contender and forcing him to the ground. The younger male fights back, pounding on the older male with his massive forearms, screaming at the top of his voice. The female launches herself at the him as well, screaming in fear and anger.

In the midst of all this chaos and violence, the *afarensis* gradually become aware of more screaming coming from just beyond the clearing. At first, they do not realize what is happening, but as several strange *afarensis* males appear before them, they understand that the rival troop has returned. Outnumbered by the intruders, the *afarensis* scream with fear. Realizing their advantage, the rival troop attacks…

AFTERMATH

It is dusk. The last, slanting rays of the sun filter through the trees and sparkle on the water's surface. All is quiet, but a trail of dark, sticky blood is testament to the violence that has just been visited on this patch of forest. Further upstream, the animal that left these marks lies face down in the water. It is the lead female, her body broken by an assault that not even the strongest of males could have survived.

There is a rustling in the trees behind the female's body and her ten year-old daughter appears, walking slowly towards the river bank. She whimpers in distress at the sight of her body. Moving over to her mother's inert form, she sees that her infant

(OPPOSITE) The female looks sadly at her mother's body. *Afarensis* faces were probably very expressive and individually distinctive.

(OPPOSITE) The bipedal *afarensis* is one of our oldest ancestors.

By standing on her own two feet, she represents the key to our future.

sister is clinging tightly to her side. Hidden in the undergrowth during the attack, the infant managed to survive the brutal assault that killed her mother. She also whimpers as her sister tries to take her away, clinging more tightly, but gently she persists and pulls the infant into her own welcoming arms. The adolescent female moves off slowly through the trees, clutching her sister tightly. The female will become a surrogate mother to her orphaned sister. Like her, she is unwilling to leave their mother, but she knows they must return to the safety of the troop before night falls. Gradually, they are lost from view among the thick undergrowth and only the still, silent body remains.

Here she lies: an ape, not particularly quick or clever, with a marginal advantage in energy use, that lived and died without ceremony in the African bush. Put this way, it seems surprising that she should play such a central a role in our human story, yet she does. Not so much because of what she and her species are now, but because of what they make possible. By standing on her own two feet, she represents the key to our future. Her hands, no longer needed for locomotion, will free those that follow her to discover other uses. Shaping tools with them, they will gradually gain control over their environment and, eventually, they will create art and herald the beginning of a truly human culture. Her bipedal stance will also release the hominid line from the constraints that keep *afarensis*'s brains small and ape-like. Future hominids will develop skills beyond her understanding, feats of imagination that she cannot possibly comprehend, and they will share these with each other, through a spoken language that allows them to inhabit their own virtual worlds of thoughts and ideas, as well as the physical, everyday world that is all *afarensis* can ever know.

Standing upright has been the first step on the way to all of us. A million years will pass before there is another. It is time to leave *afarensis* and move on.

Blood Brothers

2

Paranthropus boisei had exceptionally large jaws and massive molars.

The reed bank ripples and sways in a light breeze and dragonflies flit across the water, flashing blue and silver. The ferocious heat of midday has died away but it is still hot and very humid. On the horizon, clouds are building. Soon the rains will come and the long dry season will be at an end. At the edge of the reeds, where the receding waters have left a bank of dried-out mud, a small, sturdy ape-like animal crouches, digging into the mud with a stick. Reaching down into the hole he has made, he pulls up the muddy root of a sedge plant and, after briefly rinsing it in the water, pops it into his mouth and begins chewing. Huge muscles bulge in his jaw and cheeks as he grinds away at his food, steadily, doggedly, the mouthful of food taking almost half a minute to consume. His odd, dish-shaped face appears impassive, but he is keeping a close eye on the rest of his troop, who are strung out along the shoreline.

Turning his head, he also monitors the few troop members that are digging for food in the shade of the trees that fringe the lake. They also use sticks to dig but, instead of sedge roots, bulbs and tubers are their reward. Too far from the water to make washing an option, they rub their food against their hairy arms to dislodge dirt and grit before eating it. The only sounds to be heard are the contented grunts they make at each other, and the sound of relentless chewing, as they pulverize food between their immense molar teeth. These creatures belong to a species known as *Paranthropus boisei*, and they are australopithecines, descendants of animals like *afarensis*.

To the amazement of the *boisei*, the peace of the feeding session is broken as another two-legged creature enters the glade, running at full tilt. Like the *boisei*, he is short – around 125 centimetres (4 feet) tall at the most – with long arms and short legs, but there the resemblance ends. Unlike them, he is lightly built, and his hair is rather sparse, revealing the dark skin beneath.

He is also more finely featured, with a sloping forehead and a small, projecting snout; he lacks the huge jaws and massive facial muscles that give the others their strange concave faces. His teeth are also considerably smaller and narrower than the *boisei*'s – a hard, fibrous diet is not something he is designed to cope with – and his brain is larger. This is *Homo habilis*, and he and his kind have developed skills unseen on this planet until now.

As he vanishes through the trees on the other side of the clearing, the reason for his high-speed exit appears. They are also hominids, but taller than the dominant *habilis* male, and their long-legged build is more modern than his; all three of the pursuers run with the same easy, fluid gait. Facially too, they are distinct from *habilis*, with a large, flat face that brings to mind a much less extreme version of *boisei*. They also have much larger teeth and, intriguingly, their brains are larger as well. They belong to a species called *Homo rudolfensis*. They shout and gesture at each other as they run, clearly trying to decide which route they should take. Then they too are gone, their shouts fading in the distance.

Compared to *boisei*, *Homo habilis* was a much slighter animal, with smaller jaws and teeth.

Our journey has moved us on to East Africa, two million years before the present day. We have arrived in an extraordinary place at an extraordinary time – a time of evolutionary expansion. Over the past one and a half million years, the hominid family tree, already bushy to begin with, has blossomed into an even more fantastically rich and diverse array; there are now as many as half a dozen species roaming the wooded grasslands of East and southern Africa, each with their own strategy for survival. Unlike modern-day humans, our ancient ancestors are not alone.

What caused this remarkable explosion of hominid species? The answer lies in the gradual

It has been suggested that *boisei* may have lived in social groups with a single dominant male and several females, rather like modern gorillas.

drying of the East African climate that began over five million years ago. We have already seen how an initial dry period led to the emergence of *afarensis* from the diminishing rainforests of Africa. Around a million years later, there was another dramatic period of global cooling and drying. Triggered by changes in the Earth's orbit around the sun, the ice sheets expanded, locking up the planet's reserves of water. The expansion of the ice cap announced the beginning of a series of glacial cycles – the ice ages – that continue to the present day. Changes in fossil pollen from this period show that in East Africa there was an increase in grassland and a decline in the area of wooded savannah, while the seasons became more extreme, with marked wet and dry periods. Between 2.8 and two and a half million years ago, this window of climatic deterioration was marked by an increase in the rate at which new species appeared and went extinct, leading to what has been called a 'turnover pulse' of evolutionary change.

In East Africa, twenty-nine species of forest antelope became extinct and were replaced by species that were specialized for living in open habitats. Species previously found only in northern regions of Earth also began to appear in Africa as the planet cooled and temperate habitat types spread towards the equator. By two million years ago, a whole new suite of animals inhabited East Africa, all of which were adapted to the new range of habitats and food sources that climate change had created. And the hominids were no exception. They too diversified into a number of species, each with a unique array of adaptations that enabled them to meet the challenges that life now presented. While the *boisei* became specialized to feed on low-quality, abundant foods such as underground tubers, corms and roots, *habilis* and *rudolfensis* evolved a different strategy, varying their diet with the seasons and aiming for the highest-quality food sources they could find. Both of these strategies were highly effective, but only one proved to be resilient in the face of continued climatic change.

A NEW ARRIVAL

The disturbance over, the *boisei* return to their digging. The male returns from the reed beds and, marching over to a female who is excavating a hole full of small corms, displaces her from the spot with a mild threat. She does not move off straightaway, reluctant to sacrifice all her hard work. Her status as the dominant female of the troop, the male's first ever mate, gives her the confidence to attempt this defiant stance. The male, however, is in no mood for insolence. He shoves her off roughly and begins to dig for himself, abandoning his stick and using his powerful arms to dig deeper, throwing back huge handfuls of dirt. The hairy crest on the top of his head shows gingery red highlights as it catches the light and the same colours glint in the saddle of hair across his lower back. This marks him out as the dominant male in the troop.

Male *boisei* had large crests of bone on the top of their heads to which their chewing muscles were attached. Females with their smaller jaws, didn't need these bone protruberances.

71

Rather like modern-day gorillas, *boisei* live in small troops of a dozen or so, with a dominant male who monopolizes all the mating. The nature of their diet means that females can stay more tightly clustered together than a species such as *afarensis*, where competition for fruit forced females to keep their distance from each other to a greater degree. This clustering of the females makes it much easier for a single male to control the group, although there are always a few younger males waiting in the wings for their chance to mate.

Although male *boisei* are considerably larger than the females, the main difference in size comes not in their bodies but in the size of their skulls. Although stout and solidly built, *boisei* are still very small animals compared to modern humans – standing about 137 centimetres (4 feet 6 inches) – but, relative to their bodies, their heads and teeth are enormous. Males, in particular, have skulls over twice the size

In the *boisei* troop, the male was often the focus of the females' attention.

Paranthropus boisei

Who discovered boisei?

Paranthropus boisei was discovered by Louis and Mary Leakey in 1959, and was named after the American industrialist, Charles Boise, who helped fund the Leakeys' work. (Paranthropus means 'near man' and was named by Robert Broom, who first discovered the South African robust species.) Louis Leakey originally named the species Zinjanthropus boisei, and the type specimen, the fossil that defines and characterizes a species, OH-5, is nicknamed Zinj, although it is sometimes called Nutcracker Man due to the enormous size of its back teeth. The find was extremely important at the time since, until then, no hominid fossil sites had been dated accurately.

When did boisei live?

The age of the oldest hominid fossils in 1959 was estimated at only half a million years. The volcanic layers at Olduvai Gorge, in Tanzania, meant that the newly discovered technique of potassium-argon dating (see the feature on pages 108–9) could be used. It revealed that Zinj was a staggering 1.75 million years old, much older than anyone had ever imagined possible. The whole array of boisei fossils that have been found so far range in age from two to one million years old.

Where did boisei live?

Boisei is found only in East Africa and is known from Olduvai, and Koobi Fora (East Turkana) in Kenya. Among the first of the Koobi Fora specimens found by the team of Richard Leakey, Louis and Mary's son, were two robust fossils, KNM-ER 406 and KNM-ER 732. These species differed quite substantially in size, 732 is much smaller than 406. However, they shared the same essential features and it was initially concluded that 732 was a female boisei while 406 was a male. However, in recent years some scientists have suggested that the Koobi Fora specimens may represent a completely different species from boisei. The discovery of the black skull, Paranthropus aethiopicus (see the feature on pages 98–9), on the west side of Lake Turkana in 1985 makes this suggestion less outlandish than it might at first seem, since this find made it clear that boisei was not the only form of robust australopithecine found in East Africa.

What would boisei have looked like?

Boisei has been described as being 'hyper-robust' with extremely large jaws and teeth. Although boisei bones were stout, with thick shafts, and their skulls were large and heavy, boisei males were only 137 centimetres (around 4 feet 6 inches) tall and weighed 49 kilograms (7 stone 10 pounds), while females were much smaller, standing only 124 centimetres (4 feet 1 inch) tall and weighing only 34 kilograms (5 stone 5 pounds), only slightly larger than a modern male baboon. Essentially, they were very small animals with large heads and enormous teeth. Compared to the

Male Paranthropus boisei.

other species of robust australopithecine, the South African Paranthropus robustus, with which it overlaps in time, boisei shows more exaggerated facial features. As the number of boisei specimens has increased, it has become clear that the two species are actually very similar, and may just represent geographical variants of a single widespread species (which would be called Paranthropus robustus since this was named first).

How would boisei have lived?

The large teeth of boisei suggest it fed on very hard vegetable matter that needed a great deal of chewing, like roots and tubers. Such food was widespread and easy to find, and this vegetarian diet may have allowed them to live at higher population densities than other hominids like Homo habilis.

What a tooth can tell

Teeth are among the most common items found in the fossil record. The extreme hardness of tooth enamel means that, compared to other structures, teeth have a much higher chance of surviving intact long enough for fossilization to occur. Since teeth are the first things to come into contact with an animal's food, their structure can tell us a lot about what a species ate. Species that eat leaves, like African colobus monkeys, tend to have molars with high sharp crests that slice up plant matter into very fine pieces so that it can be fermented more effectively in the stomach. Fruit eaters, on the other hand, like chimpanzees, tend to have broader, flatter molars, since their food needs to be crushed rather than finely sliced.

The patterns of wear found on the tooth enamel can also reveal a great deal about diet. With the use of scanning electron microscopes that can detect the tiny pits and scratches on teeth, scientists have been able to show that different foods produce very characteristic toothwear patterns, so that it is possible to distinguish a grazing animal from one that browses on bushes and shrubs, or a fruit-eater from a leaf-eater. Analysing the patterns from fossil hominid teeth reveals that all the early hominids like *afarensis* fall into the fruit-eater category. Like chimpanzees, their tooth enamel is fairly smooth with a few pits and scratches. However, with the evolution of *Homo ergaster* and *erectus*, a major shift is seen. Their tooth enamel is very heavily pitted and scratched,

showing a pattern much more like that of the bone-crunching, meat-eating hyena or a rooting, eat-anything pig. While the exact nature of diet change at this point is still a matter of debate, it is clear that *ergaster* changed its feeding behaviour quite drastically compared to the other hominids. One scenario that seems likely is a switch to more efficient hunting behaviour, compared to the scavenging of *habilis*, and a greater reliance on meat as a regular part of the diet.

Tooth enamel can also be analysed for its chemical content, and this gives further clues about the nature of hominid diets. Carbon isotope analysis calculates the ratio of two different forms of carbon, carbon-13 and carbon-12, in tooth enamel and this can be used to work out the kinds of plants an animal ate. This is because plants can use two forms of photosynthesis (the process by which plants generate energy from sunlight and water); the amount of carbon-13 that is retained in the plant's structure depends on the form of photosynthesis used. Trees, shrubs and bushes use carbon-3 photosynthesis, and they tend to contain lower ratios of carbon-13. Grasses and plants like maize and sorghum are carbon-4 photosynthesizers, and they tend to have higher ratios of carbon-13. Levels of carbon-13 in the tooth enamel give a good indication of whether an animal primarily ate grass species or concentrated more on bushy plants.

The amount of carbon-13 can also

reveal how much meat a species ate. Studies of *Paranthropus robustus* teeth reveal high levels of carbon-13. Since this species was very unlikely to be a grazer – its teeth are not suited for eating grass – the high levels of carbon-13 in their teeth can only have got there because they were eating an animal that ate grass. One suggestion is that they fed on grass-eating termites, but it is also possible that *robustus* may have included a small amount of meat in its diet.

Teeth can also tell us quite a lot about a species' social system and its mating patterns. In animals where males compete for mating rights to females, the males' canine teeth are very large and sharp, projecting a long way down beyond the rest of the tooth row. They can often be twice the size of the females' canines. These blade-like canines act as weapons that the males use to fight each other and establish dominance hierarchies. The alpha male is the one that has the most mating opportunities and can mate promiscuously with all the females in the troop.

Among the hominids, both the canines and the body size differ substantially between *afarensis* males and females, indicating a considerable level of competition for mates. In *Paranthropus boisei*, the picture is rather more confusing as there are large body size differences between males and females, but there is very little difference in the

(ABOVE) An array of *afarensis* jaws and teeth from Afar, Ethiopia.

(MIDDLE) The jaw of *Homo habilis* found at Olduvai Gorge, Tanzania.

(RIGHT) The upper jaw (top) and lower jaw (bottom) of *Paranthropus boisei* showing the enormous crushing molar teeth.

size of the canine teeth between the sexes, and the canines are also very small indeed. Large body size in males suggests some degree of competition between them, although the small canine teeth contradict this. However, its possible that the evolution of the robust 'grinding machine' for chewing hard foods, which resulted in a massive increase in the size of the molars, may have meant that large canine teeth were no longer possible. There may simply not have been enough room in their mouths for both large canines and enormous molars. In this case, body size differences may be a better guide to the social system than tooth size.

Among *habilis* and the later *Homo* species, like *ergaster* and *heidelbergensis*, both canine tooth size and body size differences between males and females are greatly reduced, suggesting that male competition for mates was much lower. This is probably due to pair bonds developing between males and females, with males sticking with just one mate and helping to raise the offspring, rather than attempting to mate with all the females present in the group.

of females', which is the same level of sexual dimorphism (the difference in body size between males and females) seen in the gorilla. These huge skulls reflect the evolution of the *boisei* 'grinding machine' – an extraordinary increase in the size of the molar teeth and jaws that enables them to feed on very hard foodstuffs, like dense unyielding sedge roots. They are able to crush and grind these items extremely finely and extract every last nutrient from these coarse, low quality foods. While their incisors and canines are relatively small, *boisei* molars are over four times the size of ours, and are even bigger than those of a male gorilla, an animal almost four times their size.

These teeth are embedded in large robust jaws, and their huge grinding force is provided by two pairs of powerful chewing muscles, the masseter and the temporalis. The temporalis muscles attach to the sides of the skull and, in *boisei* males, the large size of these muscles means that there is not actually enough space to fit them on, since *boisei*'s brain is still quite small, around 520 cubic centimetres (32 cubic inches). As a result, males have developed a huge bony crest along the top of the skull – known as the sagittal crest – to which the temporalis muscles are anchored. Females, being relatively smaller, do not need extra attachment surfaces for their muscles, so they do not have crests on their heads. The other chewing muscles, the masseters, are anchored to the lower jaw and run up the side of the face where they attach to the cheek bones. When these muscles contract, they provide a massive crushing force to the back teeth. As with the temporalis, the huge size of this muscle has dramatic anatomical consequences: *boisei*'s cheekbones are powerfully built so that they can provide the substantial attachment surfaces these muscles need, and they also flare forwards so that the masseters can fit underneath them. *Boisei*'s cheekbones are pushed so far forward, in fact, that they stick out further than its nose, giving its face its characteristic 'dished' appearance.

a *boisei* troop was forced to spend most of its day digging and chewing.

The huge size of *boisei*'s molars are a good indicator that their diet consisted of small, tough items, like sedge roots and corms, but detailed analyses of the wear patterns on their teeth reveal that they also ate fruit. This suggests that *boisei* fed on high-quality fruits when it got the chance – mainly during the wet season, when fruits were most abundant – and turned to the tough, low quality items during the dry season when little else was available. This reliance on low-quality foods to see them through the hard times is probably the reason that *boisei* was so short. Even at these small body sizes, a *boisei* troop was forced to spend most of its day digging and chewing. If it were any larger, it would have needed to eat day and night in order to obtain sufficient energy. Its large head and small body may look odd to us, but together they comprised an excellent adaptation to the demands of the seasonal grasslands of East Africa.

After several hours in the glade, the *boisei*'s return on their digging efforts is diminishing, and they are pulling up far fewer edible roots and tubers. It is clear that the patch is exhausted, and already several animals are beginning to move off in search of new digging sites. The male is the last to leave but, as he goes, he spots a new face on the edge of the clearing, a female he has never seen before. Unbeknown to him, she has been watching him and the rest of the *boisei* for most of the day; she is alone and in search of a new troop to join. The male approaches, murmuring softly, his face showing an expression of interest and attraction. His bulky facial muscles means that his expressions lack subtlety,

Female *boisei* were much smaller than males with less extreme features of the face and skull.

77

(ABOVE) A snoozy *boisei* infant with his mother.

(OPPOSITE) Unlike modern humans, *boisei* eyes did not have any whites and so *boisei* lacked the ability to know what another individual was thinking just by looking into them.

but they are highly effective at getting the message across. The male walks around the new female, sniffing gently at her. The female reaches out and begins to groom his arm, tentatively, softly.

From just beyond the glade, the dominant female watches as this scene develops. A new female means more competition for the male's attentions, and she instinctively takes a dim view of these events. She strides over to the pair and grunts in greeting to the male. The new female jumps in surprise and grins at the dominant submissively, in an attempt to appease, but her hands remain buried in the male's hair and she continues grooming. The dominant female is determined to assert herself and ignores the new female's friendly overtures. She swipes the new female's hands away from the male and barks aggressively. The male in his turn threatens the dominant female, leaping up and displaying, sending her reeling backwards. The male settles again and gestures to the new female, but she is too afraid to approach, and backs away. The dominant female, rather more subserviently this time, takes her place next to the male, and begins to groom him, grunting softly and smacking her lips.

The new female trails slowly from the clearing, reluctant to leave the male, but equally reluctant to incur the dominant female's wrath. The male grunts in response to his grooming partner, but his eyes never leave the new female. The dominant female has a rival, and there seems little she can do about it.

Out in the scrubby grassland, the *habilis* male also finds that he has few options. Still pursued by the *rudolfensis* trio, he is tiring, but there is no sign of a hiding place or, indeed, the rest of his troop. Stumbling on, lacking the energy to run any faster, he can sense the *rudolfensis* gaining on him. He turns to check exactly where they are and catches his foot in a mongoose burrow. He falls heavily, winding himself and throwing up clouds of dust from the parched ground. As the dust clears, he finds himself confronted with a pair of dusty kneecaps. Gazing upwards, he looks into the wide, flat face of *rudolfensis*.

The *habilis* male has no idea why he is being chased. Accidentally separated from the rest of his troop, the male literally fell over the

rudolfensis, who were resting in the shade of the trees in the *boisei* glade. Clearly, they took his sudden appearance rather badly, but the *rudolfensis* were more surprised than anything else. In fact, they were about to give up the chase when the *habilis* fell. Now that he is stationary, however, they move in threateningly. The *habilis* male shuffles backwards through the dust, desperately trying to scramble upright. As the dust rises, a thought occurs to him and, without warning, he throws a handful of dust straight into the faces of the *rudolfensis*. The distraction works – coughing and rubbing their eyes, the *rudolfensis* are no longer interested in the *habilis*, who is on his feet again and racing off into the distance.

Retracing his steps, the *habilis* male looks for signs of his troop. He had wandered away from them in search of something more satisfying to eat than the few paltry corms that the troop had been able to dig up that morning. Although lacking the huge teeth of *boisei*, the *habilis* are able to feed on some of the smaller, more tender corms and roots that can be found underground. They are a useful stop-gap, a means of holding off hunger until something more profitable is found, but now, at the end of the dry season, their hunger is never quite satisfied, and a groaning stomach is something the young male has to live with constantly. Returning to the spot where he last saw his troop, the male can hear them not too far off. They sound excited and, despite his tiredness, the male once again breaks into a run, hopeful of what he will find.

The *habilis* are gathered round a dead, rotting tree. They gaze up towards the top and, joining them, the young male also cranes his neck and peers upward. At the top of the tree, the troop's dominant male gingerly inspects a bees' nest, hoping to find some honey, a sugary high-energy treat. Shinning up the tree trunk presented him with no problem, since *habilis*'s body proportions are still rather like those of *afarensis*, with long arms relative to their rather short legs, and they are accomplished climbers. On the ground, however, *habilis* is now indistinguishable from modern humans in the way it walks. Like modern humans, it has short, straight toes and a distinct arch to its foot.

(OPPOSITE) *Homo rudolfensis* had a face that was very like that of the earlier australopithecines, especially *Australopithecus africanus*.

(ABOVE) *Homo habilis* had rather ape-like facial features, including a protruding snout.

Although *habilis* lacked feet that could grasp, its long arms and short legs meant that it could climb with ease.

The dominant male pokes at the nest experimentally; a few bees emerge and sleepily buzz around him. Heartened by this, he pokes a hole in the nest with a digging stick, and begins fishing around inside it more confidently. However, the dry season is taking its toll on the bees as well as the *habilis*. With so few flowers around, they are unable to make honey in large quantities. More bees fly out as the male's actions prompt them to begin stinging in defence of the nest. The stings are painful and the male forgets all about honey in his desire to avoid being stung any further. Heaving at the nest, he manages to pull it from the tree and sends it tumbling through the air. As it lands, it smashes open, exploding with angry bees.

Having thrown the bees' nest ahead of him, the dominant male leaps to the ground to sort through the debris for honey.

The *habilis* troop scatter, waving their arms around their heads. The dominant male drops to the ground and, in a last-ditch effort, begins to sort through the debris in the hope of finding a least some honey that will redeem him in the eyes of the troop. The stinging is savage, however, and he is forced to retreat dejectedly, pulling stings from his arms and face.

The young male watches with a look of dismay. His stomach rumbles once again, and he feels a deep weariness in his bones. The rest of the troop begin to scratch around in the soil, pulling up some small, greasy corms that will do nothing to assuage their hunger, but the young male slumps in the shade of a rocky outcrop

The birth of bigger brains

Unlike monkeys and apes, whose infants are able to move around independently soon after they are born, humans give birth to very helpless young. This is because human babies develop very slowly in the womb and are born at a stage when they are still very under-developed compared to the ape species: the brain of human newborns is only one quarter of its full size, whereas those of chimpanzee infants are already half grown at birth. Most of a human baby's development therefore takes place outside the womb, with the brain only reaching full size at around a year of age. Being born so early is what makes human infants so uniquely vulnerable and helpless.

One of the major reasons that human babies are born so early is because of the size and structure of the mother's pelvis. For a species to walk efficiently on two legs, the pelvis must provide very stable support for the upper body and the internal organs. This has given rise to a bowl-shaped pelvis in modern humans that works very effectively as far as walking is concerned, but creates some problems for giving birth. It restricts the size of the birth canal, making it more difficult to get the baby's head and shoulders through. As well as its smaller size, the modern human birth canal is also 'twisted' in the middle, further complicating the process of giving birth. The inlet to the birth canal is widest from side to side, so the baby enters it facing sideways, with the

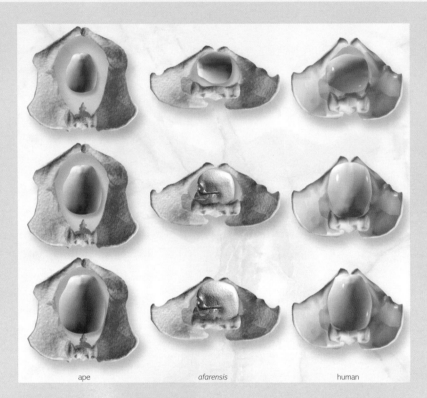

ape   afarensis   human

The ease with which an infant's head passes through the mother's birth canal depends on the size of the baby's head and the shape of the mother's pelvis. The more bowl-shaped pelvis of *afarensis* and humans means that it is a tighter fit, and the large size of the human brain means that the baby has to rotate its head halfway through birth in order to squeeze through.

widest part of its head in line with the widest part of the pelvis. However, the outlet of the birth canal is widest from top to bottom, so that halfway through birth, in order to squeeze through the outlet, the baby has to rotate so that it is facing downwards.

These pelvic complications were not a problem for the first bipedal hominids, like *afarensis*, because their pelvis was

much wider than a modern human's. As a result, their birth canal was also wide and straight all the way down with no twists in the middle. This meant that *afarensis* babies were probably born with less difficulty than modern human babies since, after entering the birth canal sideways, their heads would have passed through more easily and they would not have needed to rotate their bodies halfway down. However, *afarensis* infants may have had to rotate their bodies slightly once their head was out so that their broad shoulders were positioned facing the widest part of the mother's pelvis and could also pass through easily. *Homo habilis* probably also gave birth much like the earlier australopithecines. Even though its brain had increased in size quite substantially, it probably had a wide pelvis and birth did not involve the rotation of the baby in the birth canal, but only as the baby emerged so that its shoulders could get through.

This rotation meant that the baby was born facing away from its mother so that, if the mother looked down as the baby emerged, she would see the back of its head. In monkeys and apes, the baby emerges facing the mother, so that it is very easy for her to reach down and help guide the baby from the birth canal and clear mucus from its nose and mouth to help it breathe. With the baby's head facing away from them, australopithecine and early *Homo* females would have had great trouble helping the baby out and the risk of birth complications was greatly increased. Scientists have suggested that, to avoid these birthing problems, australopithecine females would have sought out other females who could act as 'midwives' and help them deliver the baby safely. These females would most likely have been the female's relatives, like her mother and sisters, and would have favoured the evolution of long-lasting kinship bonds between females who could help each other give birth. The fact that modern women want supportive, familiar individuals with them

when they give birth thus has deep evolutionary roots, extending right down to the very beginnings of humanity.

As brain size continued to increase from *habilis* to *ergaster* to modern humans, and the pelvis became more rounded and squat, giving birth became more problematic for the hominids, and help at the birth was not enough to solve it. Some sort of evolutionary compromise was needed to deal with the eye-watering prospect of trying to squeeze an ever larger head through an ever smaller passage.

One solution was the evolution of wider hips in females compared to males. This helps to widen the birth canal so that a larger head can pass though it. However, the amount of widening that could actually take place was very limited because it affected the ability to walk efficiently. Even the small difference that exists today between the two sexes substantially reduces female efficiency, and means that women will never be able to run a 100-metre sprint as fast as men. With the limits of female hip widening reached, the only other available solution to the problem was to give birth at a stage when the infant's brain was still very small, and its head could fit through the birth canal more easily. The helplessness of human babies was an unavoidable side effect of this compromise.

It has been calculated that this switch to the modern form of birth took place around 1.9 million years ago with the evolution of *Homo ergaster*. At this point, the infant's head would have been unable to pass through the pelvic girdle unless brain growth was slowed and the infant was born at a more helpless stage.

Giving birth in this way had profound effects on *ergaster*'s social structure. From *afarensis* to *habilis*, females would probably have been able to cope alone with their infants who, like ape infants, would probably have been able to cling and move independently quite soon after birth. With the evolution of early birth and more helpless infants, patterns of childcare would have had to change, since a female would no longer have been able to both care for her new infant effectively and move around freely gathering food for herself. It may have been at this point that male–female pair bonding first evolved, and a division of labour between the sexes became much more marked, as males went out to find food and females remained at a home base caring for the couple's offspring.

A female orang-utan and her infant. Ape babies are much more active and independent than human babies because their brains are already half-grown at birth.

and gazes off disconsolately into the distance. Almost instantly, he is on his feet again, hooting and pointing. The rest of the troop follow his gaze and see vultures wheeling in the sky. The young male is already off and running, pausing only to grab a large rock on his way out of the acacia grove.

The young male's actions reflect the increased mental capacities bestowed on him by a larger brain. They allow *habilis* to make sense of their world in an entirely new way, far beyond the understanding of their ape-like ancestors. In common with the rest of his kind, the young male understands the relationships that exist between the things he sees around him, linking them together in ways that enhance his ability to survive and exploit his habitat successfully. He knows exactly what the circling vultures mean, and he jogs off steadily in their direction, determined not to miss out.

Eager to prove himself, the young *habilis* finds a vantage point to look for possible food. *Habilis* was an opportunistic forager, always with an eye for a potential meal.

A BIGGER BRAIN

The defining mark of *Homo* is increased brain size. *Homo habilis* had an average cranial capacity of around 650 cubic centimetres (40 cubic inches), still a long way from the 1,350 cubic centimetres (82 cubic inches) of the average modern human, but a marked increase compared to the earlier australopithecines. This increase in brain size reflects the expansion of one area in particular; studies of endocasts show that, compared to the australopithecines, *habilis* had much bigger frontal lobes (the parts of the brain that sit just behind the forehead), and the pattern of wrinkles and grooves on them was the same as in modern humans. These parts of the brain are associated with higher thought processes, such as problem-solving and planning, revealing that *habilis* was capable of the kinds of abstract thought far surpassing the abilities of any australopithecine. Interestingly, large brains do not characterize all fossil specimens of *habilis*. There are some with an estimated cranial capacity of only 510 cubic centimetres (31 cubic inches) – around the same size as *boisei*. However, endocasts show that *habilis*'s brain also had a different structure from that of the australopithecines, and this change in brain organization may also account for *habilis*'s increased mental capacities, rather than the increase in size alone.

During the dry season, *habilis* would have struggled to find enough food to satisfy the whole group.

Regardless of what actually explains *habilis*'s greater mental skills, there is no doubt that they put them to good use in their ceaseless search for food – and one kind of food in particular: meat. This is especially so now, in the dry season, when fruits and other vegetable foods are in short supply. At times like these, *habilis* turns increasingly to meat scavenged from predator kills to supplement its diet, and a larger brain is a definite asset for a number of reasons. In the first place, finding fresh kills requires *habilis* to be aware of the clues available in its environment, since carcasses are widely scattered and so random searching is highly inefficient. By taking their cue from other scavengers, such as the vultures, *habilis* saves valuable search time. Second, once a carcass is located, *habilis*'s ingenuity helps it to protect its precious find against competing scavengers, such as hyenas and jackals, and also the predators themselves. Lastly, and most importantly, *habilis*'s larger brain means that it possesses a skill that enables it to exploit a carcass in ways far beyond the means of other scavengers: something that represents a major breakthrough in the hominid line, marking them out from the rest of the animal kingdom; something that the young *habilis* male had in mind when he paused to grab a stone on the way to his first decent meal for a week.

The *habilis* look into the distance as one of their troop heads off in the direction of a kill. *Habilis* had the ability to understand that circling vultures meant fresh meat.

The rest of the *habilis* party follow the young male, and soon they are perched high on a rocky outcrop overlooking the dry, scrubby plains. Below them lies the carcass of a recently killed antelope, a young eland, on which the vultures are feasting. The *habilis* troop scramble down, shouting as they go in order to drive off the vultures, their excitement at finding food overcoming caution. The young male, however, hangs back. The kill is very fresh, and he knows the predator responsible may still be close by. However, it is not necessarily a predator that he needs to watch out for…

Homo rudolfensis

Male *Homo rudolfensis*.

Who discovered *rudolfensis*?

Homo rudolfensis was established as a species in 1986 by the anthropologist Bernard Wood. The name *rudolfensis* had already been used by the Russian anthropologist V. P. Alexeev, who in 1975 suggested that the fossil KNM-ER 1470, which Richard Leakey's team had recently discovered in Koobi Fora, Kenya, should be placed in an genus of its own, named *Pithecanthropus rudolfensis,* since it was so different to the other *habilis* fossils found to date. At the time, no one was willing to accept Alexeev's suggestion, and ER 1470 was considered to be *Homo habilis*.

However, the marked differences between ER 1470 and other *habilis* fossils such as OH-7 (a partial skull from Olduvai Gorge) and KNM-ER 1813 (a skull from Koobi Fora) could not be ignored by some, including Wood; ER 1470, along with some other Koobi Fora specimens, was placed in *Homo rudolfensis*. Individual fossil specimens from Ethiopia (a tooth), Kenya (a temporal bone) and Malawi (a lower jaw bone), have also been included in *Homo rudolfensis*.

When did *rudolfensis* live?

Fossils of *rudolfensis* from Koobi Fora, have been dated to 1.9 million years ago. The other fossils from Ethiopia, Kenya and Malawi are all dated to 2.4 million years ago, around the same time that the first stone tools are found. This makes *rudolfensis* the oldest species of *Homo* currently known.

Where did *rudolfensis* live?

The species *rudolfensis* is best known from Koobi Fora, but fossils from Ethiopia and Malawi show that this species had quite a wide geographical range.

What did *rudolfensis* look like?

Rudolfensis differs from *habilis* in that it has much larger teeth, and a larger brain size of around 750 cubic centimetres (46 cubic inches). Facially, it is also very different with a narrow upper facial region and small eye sockets, but a very broad mid-facial region with flared cheekbones. These features are completely different from those of *habilis*, and some scientists have suggested that *rudolfensis* is, in fact, a large australopithecine. Indeed, an analysis comparing the facial features of ER 1470 with Zinj, the famous *boisei* skull from Olduvai Gorge, showed that they were very similar, whereas comparisons between *boisei* and *habilis* specimens, like ER 1813, showed no similarities at all.

Given these findings, some scientists have suggested that *rudolfensis* is actually an East African version of the South African species, *Australopithecus africanus*. This would certainly help explain the robust-like facial features of *rudolfensis*, since *africanus* closely resembles the robust species in a lot of ways. Other researchers, however, remain fully convinced that ER 1470 is a member of *Homo*.

Fossils other than the skull and jaw bones have not been found directly associated with *rudolfensis* skulls, which makes it difficult to be sure that they belong to the same species; but if it is assumed that they do, then compared to *habilis*, *rudolfensis* has more modern limb proportions. They were also slightly larger, standing 157 centimetres (5 feet 2 inches) tall and weighing around 52 kilograms (8 stone 4 pounds).

How would *rudolfensis* have lived?

Like *habilis*, *rudolfensis* was probably a scavenger and generalized forager. Their larger body size may have made them more effective at scaring off other animals from kills, and they may have been more successful scavengers as a result.

Habilis and *rudolfensis* confront each other. Their very similar lifestyles meant they often found themselves competing for the same resources.

The other *habilis* reach the carcass. The dominant male is there first, and drops to his knees to inspect how much meat remains. As he does so, a stinging blow to the head knocks him forwards, and he finds himself sprawled across the fly-blown eland. A large stone, now lying harmlessly in the dust, seems to have been responsible. Another stone, and then another, confirm this to be the case. Fending off the rain of stones, the male turns to see a group of *rudolfensis* silhouetted against the sky, high on the outcrop that the *habilis* troop has just left. Although they are primarily vegetarian, both *habilis* and *rudolfensis* scavenge for meat when times are hard, and the two species often find themselves in direct competition. Partly this is due to the fact that they can only feed on fairly fresh carcasses. Rotting meat makes them ill, and they are not attracted to anything that has been dead for any more than a day or so. The *rudolfensis* also saw the circling vultures and realized there was fresh meat for the taking.

The *rudolfensis* descend to the plain. The dominant *habilis* male runs forward to meet them, followed by the other males in his party. The two groups display, each trying to get the other to submit and leave, without actually coming to blows. The display intensifies but still no blows are struck. Fighting uses up expensive energy and is potentially dangerous – a wounded *habilis* or *rudolfensis* finds it hard to keep up with the rest of the troop, and cannot climb trees or cliffs to avoid danger – so males try to avoid actual fighting whenever possible. Today, however, the rewards are too great for either side to give in.

The aggression escalates and the dominant *habilis* male launches an attack on one of the *rudolfensis*. They wrestle and gouge at each other's faces, aiming for the eyes, striking blows wherever they can. The *rudolfensis* male struggles underneath the smaller but tenacious *habilis*, and manages to lever him off by pushing his feet against the *habilis*'s chest. The *rudolfensis* male gets ready to launch himself at the *habilis*, who now lies sprawled on the ground, but something catches the eye of the *rudolfensis* male and he looks up. Horrified, he shouts to the rest of his troop who, without hesitation, begin sprinting back to the rocks.

The *habilis* male shouts in victory, believing he is responsible for the retreat. Turning to the rest of his party, he sees they are also fleeing in the same direction as the *rudolfensis*. He barely has time to register a feeling of surprise before two lions leap on him from behind. Unnoticed by the brawling hominids, they have returned to their kill. The *habilis*'s skull is smashed by huge canine teeth, killing him instantly, and the lions begin to feed. As the remaining *habilis* watch from the safety of the rocks, it becomes apparent just how small and vulnerable these creatures are. Living by their wits

(ABOVE) Feasting on the eland carcass. *Habilis* scavenged from predator kills as a way of supplementing its meagre dry-season diet.

(BELOW) Despite *habilis*'s increased brain size and ingenuity, it is no match for a large predator like a lion.

Glancing up, she is startled to see that the male has followed her. Coming close, he pokes a second hole in the mound, on the opposite side to the first, and is able to grab his own termite snack before being defeated by the remorseless soldiers. Discarding the stick, he presents his shoulder to the female, and she begins to groom, nervously checking for the dominant female, but she is nowhere in sight. The male begins his sexual courtship in earnest, lip-smacking and grooming her in return, and eventually the female relaxes. As the last rays of hazy sunshine break through a storm-darkened sky, the male achieves his goal and, through the act of mating, adds a new female to his harem.

Returning with his new mate to the rest of the troop, the male begins to climb up into a tree for the night. The new female attempts to follow, but a coughing threat from the dominant female leads her

A torrential downpour heralds the end of the dry season and the *boisei* head for cover.

to abandon her attempts to share the male's night nest. Instead, she retreats to her own tree. She makes a desultory nest for herself and, despondent, settles down for the night as the first few drops of rain begin to fall.

The male, meanwhile, decides that making a nest is too much effort, and makes his way over to the dominant female, intending to share hers. She refuses to make way for him, and her dominant status, plus her animosity to the new female, means the male is reluctant to push her any further. Moving slowly through the massive branches, he approaches another female and another, but their nests are small and the male cannot fit. Finally, as the rain begins to fall in earnest, the male forces himself into the nest of the lowest ranking female, squashing her and her infant in the process. Despite these efforts, most of him remains hanging out of the nest but, seemingly oblivious to his ludicrous situation, the male settles down for the night.

The next morning, the *boisei* awake to a water-drenched world. The grassy clearing is festooned with rain-sparkled spiderwebs and the *boisei*'s digging holes form small pools of water from which birds flit to and fro, bathing and drinking. The male *boisei* climbs down slowly and shakes himself. His night was long, wet and miserable. In need of some grooming

(OPPOSITE AND LEFT) Some shelter from the weather is found among the tall grasses although the single stem held over his head has little effect.

(BELOW) Grooming helped the male to keep the peace and make sure the *boisei* troop stayed together.

to help him dry off and warm up, he moves over to the tree where the dominant female slept. Climbing up, he pokes at the dark, hairy body that still lies asleep. It stirs, and the dominant female's face appears over the edge of the nest. The male grunts in greeting, and then gives a start as another hairy *boisei* head appears. The new female grunts sleepily at the male, and then at the dominant female. The ferocity of the storm disintegrated the new female's paltry effort of a nest, and forced her to seek shelter in a new tree. She was apprehensive when she heard the soft grunts of the dominant female inviting her to approach but, not wanting to spend a night in the rain, she took up the offer. Now it seems that her problems are over; having gained the dominant female's acceptance, her new life in a new troop can begin. It is the male who now has to appease the dominant female, and, smacking his lips together softly, he begins to groom her, his cold, damp fingers gently searching through her thick, coarse hair.

The black skull

The evolution of the australopithecines was once thought to be a fairly simple matter; the early South African species, *Australopithecus africanus* (the Taung child – see the feature on pages 44–5), evolved into the later, more robust species *Paranthropus robustus*, which then evolved into the 'hyper-robust' *Paranthropus boisei* of East Africa. The evolutionary pathway taken was apparently clear: a steady increase over time in the size of the teeth, face and jaws of these three species. There was something of a problem with this simple scenario, however, in that *robustus*, the supposed ancestor of *boisei*, was probably younger than its supposed descendant. But it was a discovery on the west side of Lake Turkana, Kenya, in 1985 by Alan Walker, a leading palaeoanthropologist from Pennsylvania State University, that put paid to this simple story once and for all. His find, known as the 'black skull' because it was stained almost coal black, was enormously robust, even more so than *boisei*, yet it was two and a half million years old – half a million years older than any *robustus* or *boisei* specimen.

This obviously raised a difficult question: how could *boisei* be the end product of an evolutionary line for increasingly robust features when, right at the beginning of that line, there was already a fossil with all the features found in *boisei*? What is more, when examined in detail, it became apparent that, although the face was very like that of *boisei*, the back of the head was most like that of *afarensis*. Also, like *afarensis*, it had a very projecting face, with a much more pronounced snout than the later robust species (although some scientists argue that this is only because the first reconstructions of the skull positioned the facial bones too low down on the skull. If the face were placed further back on the skull, it would look much more like the other species). In other words, the most likely ancestor of this species was not *africanus*, like the other robust species, but the earlier and more primitive *afarensis*. These unique differences between the black skull and the other robust species resulted in it being placed in new species, *Australopithecus aethiopicus*.

Unsurprisingly, *aethiopicus* created rather a stir in the world of human evolution. In order to try and make sense of things, experts juggled around the relationships of all the australopithecines involved, trying to find a family tree that would allow them all to fit together neatly in a way that made sense. However, this turned out to be extremely difficult, and a satisfactory family tree with which everyone could agree proved very elusive.

Consequently, some researchers came up with a more radical solution. They suggested that *aethiopicus* was not related to any of the later robust species, but was a member of a species that died out early on and played no role in the evolution of *robustus* and *boisei*.

According to this argument, the reason that *aethiopicus*, *robustus* and *boisei* show the same flared cheekbones and large teeth is because they all needed to have powerful chewing abilities, and not because they are closely related. In much the same way, dolphins and fish both have a streamlined body shape because they both live in the sea, and not because one is descended from the other. However, the chewing adaptation may have been needed for different reasons. While *boisei* was a small animal that needed powerful jaws to cope with its hard diet, *aethiopicus* needed them because it was a big animal.

Calculations made from the size of the ulna, one of the lower arm bones, suggest that the males of this species stood around 175 centimetres (5 feet 9 inches) tall and weighed 90 kilograms (over 14 stone). Females, however, were much smaller, weighing in at around 50 kilograms (8 stone). This increase in body size alone is enough to account for the great increase in the size of chewing apparatus: *aethiopicus* has the chewing apparatus one would expect for an *afarensis*-like animal that had doubled in size from 45 to 90 kilograms (7 to 14 stone). Unlike *boisei*, its jaws and teeth are not a specially designed adaptation, but a consequence of the fact that, as its overall body size increased, so did the size of its chewing apparatus. Interestingly, however, *aethiopicus* has a very small brain, smaller even than *afarensis*, and much smaller than *boisei*.

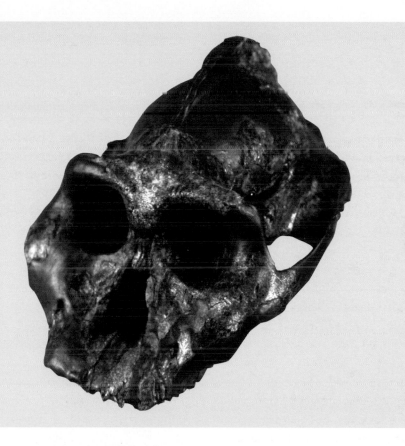

Australopithecus aethiopicus, also known as the 'black skull' because of its dark colour. The huge sagittal crest on top of its skull and its thick, flared cheekbones reveal that, like *boisei*, this species was designed for eating tough, hard-to-chew foods.

The reasons that *aethiopicus* evolved such a large body size are not entirely clear, but the most likely explanation is that it was a response to the drier conditions that arose around two and a half million years ago. A large animal can survive on much poorer quality food than a small one. Small animals have very fast metabolic rates so they need high-quality, easily digested foods to help keep them ticking over because they use up their fuel so quickly. A large animal has a slower metabolic rate, so it can take in large amounts of poor quality food and digest it slowly to extract all the available nutrients. *Aethiopicus's* large body size helped it to colonize the new savannah habitats of two and a half million years ago because it did not need to rely on high-quality fruits and berries to survive. Half a million years later, *boisei* adopted the same low-quality diet, but large body size was no longer an advantage. This was probably because their hard-to-chew diet was even tougher than that of *aethiopicus* – each mouthful needed to be chewed for up to thirty seconds in order to grind it finely enough. There just were not enough hours in the day for *boisei* to be able to eat enough food to support a body as big as *aethiopicus's*.

With the discovery of *aethiopicus*, it was no longer possible to think of hominid evolution as a simple progression of species, one after the other in a straight line. It showed that the hominid family tree was, in fact, very bushy, with side-branches and off-shoots that played no part in the evolution of later species, including modern humans, but which reflected periods of intense change, when many different species evolved in response to radical changes in the climate.

Boisei may look rather odd to us, but they were superbly adapted to their hard-chewing way of life.

A SPECIALIZED WAY OF LIVING

For *boisei*, the trials of life arise mainly from the complexities of living in a tight-knit social group: how to form relationships, find mates, raise offspring and, in the case of the dominant male, keep the peace between his females. Their superb adaptations to their diet, and the ease with which they can find the food they need, means that *boisei* life is rarely filled with the kinds of trauma that dog the *habilis*. Life for the most part remains the same, day in and day out, and as a result *boisei* is not especially innovative. Unlike *habilis*, who needs to be alive to all possible opportunities that come its way, *boisei* can stick to what it knows best. Such specialization is not to be confused with dullness or a lack of intelligence. Indeed, *boisei* brain size actually increased over time; later fossil specimens have brains so much larger than the early fossils that they no longer display a sagittal crest in the males – their skull alone was big enough to allow for the attachment of the temporalis muscles. However, such a highly specialized diet and lifestyle means that *boisei* has less ability to cope with changes to its environment – it has gone too far down one evolutionary pathway to change its ways with any ease. And this will prove to be its downfall.

Over the next few hundreds of thousands of years, the dramatic climatic changes that shaped *boisei*'s environment are set to continue. The climate will become increasingly erratic, swinging from hot to cold in a series of ice ages, and the landscape will continue to undergo tremendous geological change: change that will mean extinction for many species. Sadly, *boisei* is one of them.

Boisei's specialized lifestyle may have been its evolutionary downfall as it was unable to adapt in the face of climatic change.

Despite its behavioural complexity and its feeding specializations, *boisei* will not be here a million years from now. The reasons for their extinction are not entirely clear. Perhaps the change of climate reduced the number of reed beds available, so that their dry-season, root-eating strategy failed them. Perhaps competition with the other hominid species for high-quality vegetable foods increased, so that *boisei* had to rely more heavily on their poor-quality alternatives, even during the wet season, and in the end they simply ran out of time, unable to spend enough hours each day feeding in order to get the energy they needed.

the only *boisei* around today are the ones we see fossilized in a museum.

Whatever the reason, the only *boisei* around today are the ones we see fossilized in a museum. But this does not mean that they had no part to play in the human story. For without *boisei*, the early species of humans may never have evolved. The presence of *boisei* two million years ago meant that the ancestors of *Homo* were denied the opportunity to occupy the same vegetarian niche, and were forced to evolve alternative means of coping with the new habitats of East Africa – an opportunistic, 'try-anything' strategy. Without *boisei* providing them with indirect competition for resources, they may never have evolved the technological skills and social patterns that have shaped the pattern of human evolution ever since. They may not be our direct ancestors, but *boisei* are still one of the reasons that we are all here today.

HABILIS'S SECRET WEAPON

High on the rocks, the remaining *habilis* continue to watch the lions feed until it is too dark to see. Unsure what to do without the dominant male, they settle down to sleep where they are. They are safe on the cliffs and huddle close together for warmth. With empty stomachs, sleep takes a long time to come. But the young male is more hopeful than the rest. Less distracted by the dominant male's demise than the others, he has noticed the huge storm clouds

building on the horizon and he knows that rain is on its way, bringing the dry season to an end.

The storm lasts all night and, when morning comes, the *habilis* sit on the cliffs, small and bedraggled, gazing down longingly at the eland carcass. The lions are still there; one is asleep while the other gnaws lazily on the remains of the *habilis*. While the rain signals that a new flush of growth will soon begin, the *habilis* need food right now, and the eland remains their best bet, even though most of the meat has now gone, picked clean by the vultures. The lack of

Rocky outcrops provided *habilis* with safe, well-protected sleeping sites.

meat is not a problem, because the *habilis* are after something else: the sticky marrow inside the bones. Its high fat content means it satisfies their hunger quickly and it also serves a physiological need, because fat is needed in order to digest protein. Without a good supply of fat in their diet, the *habilis* would not be able to eat even the small amount of meat remaining on the carcass, as they would have to use their own body fat reserves to digest it – defeating the object of eating the meat in the first place. Extracting the fatty

(OPPOSITE) Tightly huddled together as a way of conserving heat, the *habilis* group gets some sleep.

(ABOVE) The hungry *habilis* continue their scavenging in search of a decent meal.

105

Habilis used stone tools to crack open bones and extract the fatty, nutritious marrow.

marrow is one of the keys to their survival, but it is not easy to get at and few other animals are able to exploit it. But *habilis* has a secret weapon.

Squatting on the cliffs of the outcrop, the young male picks up the stone he brought with him the day before. Selecting another stone from those scattered around him, he tests its weight in his hand and adjusts his grip. Making sure he is holding both stones firmly, the male brings his arm down, striking one stone against the other. A large flake chips off the stone that was struck and falls to the ground. Adjusting his grip again, the male strikes another flake from the core stone, and then another. The male sits back and inspects the object he has just made; it is a stone chopper, crude but highly effective – a tool that he can use to smash open the bones of an eland and extract the tasty, rich marrow. The flakes, with their sharp edges, can cut through flesh and sinew easily, allowing *habilis* to dismember a carcass, removing the meat and marrow-bearing bones from a kill and transporting them somewhere safe for feeding. The precarious, scavenging lifestyle of *habilis* has bred into them a remarkable ingenuity and resourcefulness which, combined with their advanced reasoning skills, gives them the power to overcome their inherent disadvantages as meat-eaters. Lacking the sharp teeth and claws that allow other animals to feed on animal prey, *habilis* have solved the problem by making tools that will do the job for them.

The significance of this development cannot be underestimated. While *boisei* may use digging sticks, these do not require a very deep understanding of tool-making. It is easy to see how a leafy stick can be turned into something suitable for digging by stripping off the leaves and small stems. It is another matter entirely to understand that by striking a shapeless lump of rock at the right angle, and with the right force, a sharp-edged blade can be produced.

Experiments performed in the United States with a captive bonobo chimpanzee named Kanzi – famous for his skills at learning some aspects of human language – have demonstrated that the skills needed to fashion tools like those of *Homo habilis* are beyond the reach of modern apes. The experimenters showed Kanzi how to strike flakes from a stone core in order to cut through a rope and lower down a basket that contained a tasty food reward. Despite a perfect understanding of what the task involved, Kanzi was never able to grasp the technique needed to produce a usable flake. In the end, he used his own technique, throwing the stones on to the hard concrete floor and smashing flakes off them that way.

As well as mental agility, the stone tools of *habilis* also indicate increased levels of manual dexterity. The hand bones of *habilis* have straight fingers with broad tips that are well supplied with nerve endings, increasing their sensitivity. One of their thumb bones also has a broad head, compared to *afarensis* and modern apes. This is associated with the fine precision grip of modern humans, and it seems that, like us, *habilis* is also able to grasp objects between the tips of the thumb and the other fingers – an attribute that is crucial for effective stone toolmaking.

With this combination of dexterity and inventiveness, *habilis* was able to produce a whole tool-kit. These make up what is known as the 'Oldowan Industrial Complex', named after the Olduvai Gorge in Tanzania where some of the largest assemblages of these tools have been found. As well as flakes and choppers, there are hammerstones (rocks that were battered against other hard objects, often other stones, to produce the flakes), coreforms (the pebble and rock fragments that flakes were struck from) and manuports (pieces of rock that were carried to a place but were not modified). There is also evidence that *habilis* further worked flakes and cores after their initial manufacture in

Without the ability to plan ahead, *habilis* made tools only in response to the situation he found himself in.

Putting hominids in their place

In order to plot the path from australopithecine to human, we need to know exactly when and where each species lived. Scientists have developed a number of ingenious ways to date fossil hominids. One very accurate method involves dating the layers of hardened ash, known as 'tuffs', which are produced as the result of a volcanic eruption. Within a sequence of rocks there are usually several tuffs, the oldest layers at the bottom and the youngest on the top. With a sequence of dated tuffs, it is possible to work out an age bracket for when a fossil animal died, with the oldest possible age being represented by the layer lying below the fossil and the youngest possible age represented by the layer lying on top of it.

The age of a volcanic tuff can be determined using a method called potassium-argon dating. This technique makes use of the fact that potassium-40, a rare, radioactive form of potassium, which makes up about 0.01 per cent of all the potassium found in rock, gradually decays over time and is converted into argon-40, a stable, inert gas. Rocks that contain potassium therefore accumulate argon as they age. The key thing that makes potassium-argon dating so useful is that, when rocks are heated to extremely high temperatures, as happens during volcanic eruptions, all the argon is driven out of them. This action is like setting a stopwatch to zero. When the rock cools, the stopwatch starts ticking as argon levels begin to build up again.

From this point on, the rock holds an accurate record of how much time has passed since the eruption. Since the amount of time it takes for a given amount of potassium-40 to decay to half its original amount (its 'half-life') is known precisely, by measuring the amount of stable potassium in the rock (which gives an estimate of the original amount of radioactive potassium that was present) and comparing it to the amount of argon that exists, it is possible to calculate exactly how long ago the eruption happened and, therefore, how old the rock layer is.

If a fossil is found in sediments where there are no tuffs that can be dated, more indirect methods can be used. One way is to look at the other animal fossils that are found with the hominid. Certain groups of animals, in particular the elephants, pigs and horses, have very detailed fossil records, with species appearing and going extinct in distinctive patterns. These sequences have all been dated accurately in areas where there are tuffs available, which means that they can be used to estimate the age of other fossils in areas where the rocks themselves cannot be dated. For example, if a fossil hominid is found in association with a fossil pig that is known to have lived, say, between two million and one and a half million years ago, it means that the hominid must also have been alive at some point during that band of time. Usually, a fossil is associated with a whole range of pig,

2 million years ago

dead hominid

tuff 1 laid down 2.1 million years ago

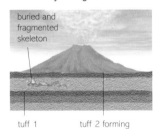

1.8 million years ago

buried and fragmented skeleton

tuff 1   tuff 2 forming

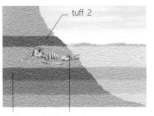

present day

tuff 2

tuff 1   fossils eroding out from the rock

The process by which layers of ash, known as 'tuffs', form in sedimentary rock. This allows fossil remains to be dated accurately by measuring the levels of radioactivity in the ash layers.

horse and elephant species, which allows the time period to be narrowed down considerably, increasing the precision of the date, since a particular combination of species is usually

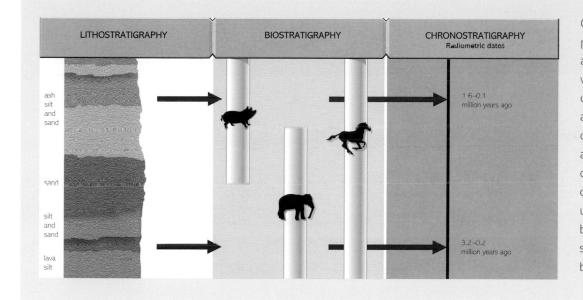

LITHOSTRATIGRAPHY	BIOSTRATIGRAPHY	CHRONOSTRATIGRAPHY Radiometric dates

ash
silt
and
sand

sand

silt
and
sand

lava
silt

1 6–0.1 million years ago

3.2–0.2 million years ago

Chronostratigraphy means placing rock layers in order of age. Rocks are aged in this way using potassium-argon dating of volcanic tuffs. In areas where this form of dating is not possible, the appearance and extinction of animal species in a distinctive sequence can be used to date fossil hominids, by matching up the sequence to the dates given by the chronostratigraphy.

associated with a much narrower time-frame than a single species.

As well as knowing when a species lived, it is also useful to know something about the habitat it lived in. Reconstructing past environments can be combined with the study of a fossil's anatomy to give important clues about an animal's ecology. On the largest possible scale, global patterns of climate change can give a rough idea of whether a habitat was very wet or very dry, and therefore the kind of vegetation it supported. This can be done using cores taken from the deep-sea floor. These cores contain tiny creatures called foraminifera. By measuring the oxygen content of their shells, it is possible to work out past climates. This is because oxygen can take several forms, one of which, oxygen-18, is much heavier than the others. When a great deal of water becomes locked up in ice-sheets during

cold periods, the sea becomes much richer in oxygen-18, and more of it is incorporated into foraminifera shells. By measuring the ratio of oxygen-18 to oxygen-16, one of the other forms of oxygen, in the shells, it is possible to tell whether the ice sheets were growing (high oxygen-18) or receding (low oxygen-18), and so whether the Earth as a whole was undergoing a period when the climate was cool and dry or hot and wet respectively.

Fossil pollen and plant fossils can also give a good idea of what a habitat was like. Plants tend to have quite a limited range of conditions in which they can live so, by identifying the plants present in a habitat, it is possible to have a good idea of what climate conditions were like at the time. It also provides information on whether a habitat was forested (a lot of tree pollen) or more open (more grass and herb pollen). The animal fossils

present can also give some clues along these lines. By identifying the fossil species and then comparing them to their modern counterparts, it is possible to work out the ecology of the extinct species: what they were likely to eat and the kind of habitat they preferred, for example. So if an array of fossil animals contains a lot of grazing species, then it is likely that the habitat was open and contained a lot of grass. If, on the other hand, the animals were browsers that tended to feed on more woody vegetation, then it is likely that the habitat was bushier and more closed.

The number of different species present can also be informative. In modern-day environments, only forest habitats contain more than four primate species living together, so if a fossil array contains more or less than this number, it can be used as a pointer to the type of habitat that was present at the time.

Habilis knapped stone tools with great efficiency, although the tools they produced were rather crude and basic.

order to improve their effectiveness. Many flakes have been retouched along one edge, and these are termed 'scrapers'. Choppers can also have flaking on both surfaces instead of just one, and these are known as 'bifacial' choppers.

In most cases, however, *habilis*'s tools are crude and uneven, and their final shape seems to have been determined by the initial shape of the rock, rather than by an idea in the head of the toolmaker. Although they have made the massive conceptual leap needed to make tools, *habilis* is not a particularly skilled toolmaker. As a result, the different kinds of tools tend to grade into one another, rather than forming completely distinct types.

Habilis also makes tools as and when they are needed, rather than using the same ones over and again. Their only signs of forward thinking are the manuports, which suggest that *habilis* carries certain kinds of rocks with them when out scavenging, perhaps because these are the most suitable for toolmaking. But, regardless of their crudeness, the stone tools of early *Homo* show us that our ancestors had reached a new level of intelligence and understanding. With this truly extraordinary invention, the first toolmakers have set humanity off on a path that will culminate in such mind-boggling achievements as the digital computer and the test-tube baby.

Using stone tools allowed *habilis* to feed on those parts of an animal, like the bone marrow, that were difficult for many other predators and scavengers to get at.

FOOD FOR THOUGHT

Grasping his freshly minted stone chopper, the young *habilis* male rounds up the rest of the troop. They also have freshly made tools and are ready to eat. Peering down at the carcass, they see the lions are still there. They have not moved off in search of fresh meat as the *habilis* hoped. While most of the troop gaze down gloomily, the young male stares into space, apparently deep in thought.

Stone tools also meant that *habilis* could remove bone and flesh from a carcass and take it to somewhere safe to eat.

A moment later, he jumps up and, grabbing another lump of rock, begins to bang it against the stone chopper noisily. Deciding this is not quite noisy enough, he begins to yell, and he also throws more rocks down towards the lions for good measure. The other *habilis* get the idea and they join in with the male's noisy display, which is clearly designed to scare the lions away from the kill.

Still yelling, the young male then surprises everybody by leaping off down the rocks, straight towards the lions. Less sure this time, the other *habilis* follow suit, and the raucous mob descends on the lions, which take flight, unsure of what to make of it all. With some relief, the male sees that his risky gambit has worked. Usually only the larger *rudolfensis* can use this tactic to see off large predators, but the sheer desperation of the *habilis* to get at some food has brought success on this occasion.

Falling on the carcass, the *habilis* begin to saw away at the eland's large back legs with their flakes and choppers. Severing them from the carcass, they retreat back up the rocks to safety, where they begin smashing open the bones with hammerstones, picking out the marrow with the ends of their sharp flakes. It is rich, sticky and delicious and the *habilis* chatter and grunt happily as they eat their fill.

Habilis individuals would share their food with each other.

Foraging together was one way of forming bonds, but nothing beat an intense grooming bout for forging friendships.

The young male in particular is exhausted but content. His skills in driving off the lions and ensuring a decent meal for the troop means that most of the other *habilis* are treating him with a new deference, particularly the females, who are keen to offer him the juiciest pieces of marrow they can find.

If the young male can capitalize on this, his future as the dominant male in the troop seems assured. Unlike his ape ancestors, skill and ingenuity are more important attributes for gaining position than sheer brute strength. With the harsh dry season over, the life of the *habilis* troop will be easier, and the young male is sure that his foraging skills will stand him in good stead during the coming months. The dangers and hardships of the past few months forgotten, the *habilis* suck contentedly on their marrow bones, and begin to look forward to the lush possibilities of the wet season.

Habilis has taken the next step towards modern humanity. Its adaptability and tool-using skills means that it has begun to free itself from the rules governing all other species on Earth. It is beginning to gain control of its environment. But despite these skills, *habilis* will not be the species that dominates Africa over the millennia to come. For another human species is emerging on the savannahs of Africa two million years before the present day – a species that also makes stone tools, but tools that are of extraordinary beauty and design, revealing a subtlety and skill far beyond the means of *habilis*. This species has a larger brain than *habilis* and possesses a more advanced array of mental skills. It is the first species that we clearly recognize as being like us, as being human. Its name is *Homo ergaster*.

Homo habilis

Who discovered *habilis*?

Homo habilis is another species discovered by Louis and Mary Leakey at Olduvai Gorge in Tanzania. Unlike the beautiful *boisei* skull known as Zinj the *habilis* remains from Olduvai are very fragmentary and there are few post-cranial bones (bones other than the skull bones and jaws). Unusually, the stone tools found associated with the fossils have been included in the species definition so that, rather than being defined purely on anatomical grounds, *Homo habilis* is partly defined by its behaviour. The discovery of stone tools was the inspiration for the name, *Homo habilis*, which literally means 'handy man'.

When did *habilis* live?

The *habilis* fossils found at the famous sites of Olduvai Gorge and Koobi Fora have been dated to 1.9 to 1.8 million years ago.

Where did *habilis* live?

Habilis fossils have been found mainly at the sites of Olduvai Gorge, Tanzania, and Koobi Fora, Kenya. In South Africa, a fossil known as Stw 53 from Sterkfontein Cave is also considered by some to be *Homo habilis*, but this belief is mainly due to its association with stone tools, rather than because of the anatomy of the fossil. Habitat reconstructions suggest that *habilis* lived in more open environments, with much more grassland, than earlier species such as *afarensis*.

What would *habilis* have looked like?

As a species, *habilis* is defined by its increased brain size (around 630 cubic centimetres, 38 cubic inches) and its smaller teeth compared to the australopithecines. The arm and leg bones associated with OH-62 (known as Lucy's child after being discovered by Donald Johanson, who also found the famous *afarensis* fossil) have very ape-like proportions, with long arms and short legs, which suggest that *habilis* still retained some tree-climbing abilities, and that these were only lost with the evolution of *Homo ergaster* around 1.8 to 1.7 million years ago. Other important post-cranial bones are the hand bones associated with a juvenile skull (OH-7, known as Jonny's child after the Leakeys' son), which show features indicating that *habilis* was capable of making the Oldowan stone tools. Fossil foot bones (OH-8) from Olduvai Gorge indicate that *habilis* had an entirely modern form of bipedalism, with a big toe in line with all the others and an arch to the foot. Using these leg and foot bones to estimate stature, *habilis* is thought to have stood around 125 centimetres (4 feet) tall and weighed 32 kilograms (5 stone). By modern human standards, *habilis* was very short indeed. Both *habilis* and *rudolfensis* show much less difference in body size between the sexes than *afarensis* and *boisei*, reflecting reduced competition for mating by males.

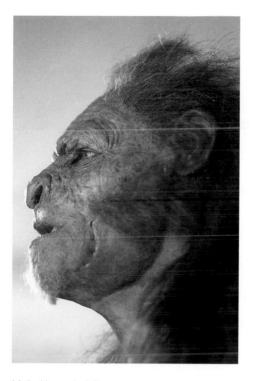

Male *Homo habilis*.

How would *habilis* have lived?

Homo habilis probably lived in fairly large groups composed of a number of males and females, plus their offspring. It was an opportunistic forager, and probably ate nuts, berries, underground corms and scavenged meat. However, it was unlikely to have tackled the tough roots eaten by *boisei* as it did not have such enormous teeth. Its ability to make and use stone tools was a crucial element of *habilis*'s scavenging strategy. This enabled it to take meat away from the site of a kill to a safer location where it was at less risk of running into predators, and it also allowed *habilis* to get at the marrow inside the bones – a part that few other scavengers could access, and which provided it with a rich, fatty food when others resources were scarce.

How many *Homo*?

Ever since it was first discovered and described, *Homo habilis* has been a controversial species. Louis Leakey, who discovered the fossils at Olduvai Gorge in Tanzania in 1961, was convinced that it was *Homo* because they were found with stone tools and, as far as he was concerned, only a human could make such items. However, there was something of a problem with this, as the estimated brain capacity of the fossil was 640 cubic centimetres (39 cubic inches) whereas, at the time the fossils were found, a figure of 750 cubic centimetres (46 cubic inches) was considered to be the 'cerebral rubicon' – the brain size that had to be reached before a species could be considered human.

In order to get round this, Leakey and his colleagues, John Napier and Philip Tobias, redefined the cerebral rubicon and decided that a brain size of 600 cubic centimetres (37 cubic inches) should mark the boundary of human brain size, thus allowing their fossil a comfortable entry into the human world.

Obviously, some scientists felt that this was moving the goalposts to suit Leakey's notions about what made a human. Besides the increase in brain size, and some changes in the size of the teeth, there was nothing, aside from the tools, that really set *habilis* apart from an australopithecine. The fossils that made up *habilis* – a partial skull, a jaw bone and some hand and foot bones – were fragmentary and could be interpreted in several different ways. Indeed, some researchers today think that there is nothing to warrant *habilis* being a member of *Homo*, and argue that its name should be changed to *Australopithecus habilis*.

It was not until the late 1960s and early 1970s that *Homo habilis* was fully accepted as a species as a result of finds made by Louis Leakey's son, Richard, at East Turkana in Kenya. The fossil that helped convince everybody – KNM-ER 1470, a 1.9-million-year-old partial skull – had a large brain size of around 750 cubic centimetres (46 cubic inches), and was safely in the realms of *Homo*. However, its face was flat, with forward projecting cheekbones, and it looked very much like an australopithecine. Despite this, many scientists were delighted by ER 1470, because here was a distinctive hominid fossil that could put a face to the name of *habilis*, which up until then had been hard to picture due to the fragmentary nature of the Olduvai Gorge fossils. This seemed a very practical solution to the problem of *habilis* and most people accepted it, although it was not very scientific reasoning, to say the least.

A subsequent find threw everything into confusion again. In 1973, another skull was found, KNM-ER 1813, which was the same age as ER 1470. Unlike ER 1470, however, this fossil had a small brain size, barely 500 cubic centimetres (30 cubic inches), but a very human-like face. Leakey thought it looked most like *Australopithecus africanus*, but Clark Howell, an American anthropologist, suggested it was, in fact, a female *Homo habilis*. He suggested that its marked difference from ER 1470 was due to the fact that ER 1470 was a male specimen. If this were the case, it meant that *habilis* had the highest sex difference in body size among the whole of the primates, including the modern gorilla. Some thought this level of sexual dimorphism was too high to justify a single species, and believed that ER 1813 could not belong to the same species as *habilis*, but again this practical suggestion seemed to suit most people.

This lasted until 1985, when Donald Johanson, working at Olduvai Gorge, found OH-62, the fragments of a female skeleton. When these were reconstructed, they showed something very surprising indeed. Although the roof of the mouth was very like that of *habilis*, OH-62 was extremely ape-like in terms of its body proportions, with long arms and short legs. It was also tiny, standing only 100 centimetres high (just over 3 feet), even shorter than *afarensis*. Once again, things had become confusing. Was this a *habilis*? And if so, how could it be so very different from both ER 1813 and ER 1470?

At this point, a number of researchers realized that *Homo habilis* had become a 'wastebasket' of a species into which a variety of different hominids had been placed, regardless of the stark differences that existed between them. Many people started referring merely to 'early *Homo*', rather than *Homo habilis*, in order to get away from the notion that there was just one species. While it was clear that Louis Leakey and his colleagues had indeed been right in naming *habilis* as a new species, it was also clear that just one species would no longer be sufficient.

Bernard Wood, a British palaeoanthropologist, rose to the challenge presented by the wide variety of *habilis* fossils. He decided that all the specimens from Olduvai Gorge belonged to *Homo habilis*, including the very ape-like OH-62; but at East Turkana, the site where ER 1470 and ER 1813 were found, Wood decided that two species were present. He assigned one group, which included ER 1813, to *habilis*, and the other, including ER 1470, to a new

species, *Homo rudolfensis*. So, at 1.9 million years ago, there were now two species roaming the plains: *habilis*, with a small brain and quite primitive body proportions, and *rudolfensis*, with a larger brain and a more modern body, but a very australopithecine-like face.

Richard Leakey, on the other hand, saw things rather differently, arguing that OH-62 was different from all the other Olduvai *habilis* fossils, and that it was therefore a completely different species from either *habilis* or *rudolfensis*. Not everyone is convinced that *rudolfensis* is a real species either, since the palate of OH-64, a *habilis* specimen from Olduvai, fits perfectly into upper jaw of ER 1470. This suggests that ER 1470 could, in fact, be *habilis*, and if so, then *rudolfensis*

would no longer exist as a species. Rather, it would be OH-62, and other fossils like it, that required recognition and a new species name. It seems confusion still reigns despite Wood's best efforts.

The number of species present and their relationships to each other will obviously need more time and more fossils to work out fully. However, the patterns that we can see today once again illustrate that this period of human evolution was not a simple, straightforward progression from the australopithecines to *Homo*, but was a time of evolutionary experimentation, in which many diverse species were present, competing with each other and influencing the path of subsequent evolution in subtle but far-reaching ways.

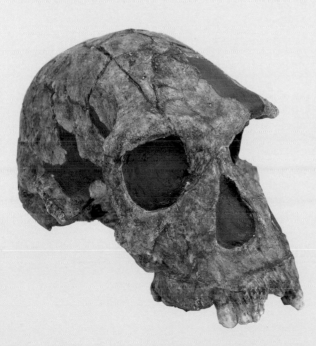

The skull known as ER 1813 is quite small brained but has a human-like face

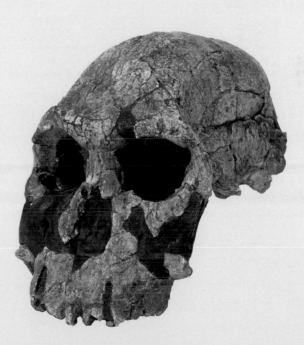

The famous ER 1470 skull has a much larger brain size than 1813 but its face is much more like that of an australopithecine.

Savage Family

3

It is the middle of the day. The sun blazes overhead in a clear sky. A vast dried mudflat stretches away as far as the eye can see, the air above it shimmering in the relentless heat and the cracked ground burning to the touch. But the creature pacing on the baking surface does not notice the scorching temperature. He is walking steadily and evenly, unfeeling of any possible pain beneath his feet, focused on one thing only: his prey.

In the far distance a lone wildebeest is moving slowly. It is old and tired, and nervous. Separated from its herd, it is exposed and in danger, but here on the baking mudflat it has found a respite from the heat. A small, muddy waterhole is offering the animal a chance of recovery, but it cannot linger here long, for it knows that it is being stalked.

This is East Africa one and a half million years ago, and here the evolution of the hominid line has taken another extraordinary step. It is as if human beings as we think of them have at last emerged on Earth. The wildebeest is being stalked by a creature called *Homo ergaster,* and the difference between his appearance and that of the little *Homo habilis* that had already emerged before him is immediately striking.

Even the feet taking *ergaster* on his relentless pursuit are clearly human in almost every detail: slim, long, toes reaching forward – feet that would not be out of place on a modern long-distance runner. The lower legs are long and slim too, supporting knees like our own, and long muscular thighs. Perfected by evolution, after more than two million years of upright walking in primates, these are the limbs of a tall human. His hips are narrow, his stomach flat, taut and strong, his chest widening above it, breathing steadily, calmly and not panting. His spine is straight; his shoulders broad, and at his sides hang long slender arms with narrow grasping fingers. His skin is a dark olive colour, smooth but with a gentle downy hair on limbs and chest that would seem normal today. This is no hairy ape-man. He stands almost 200 centimetres (over six feet) tall, with all the physical attributes needed for his environment: an African at home in his harsh domain.

Viewed at a distance, *ergaster* could easily be mistaken for modern humans.

Yet at the top of this very human body there rests a distinctly un-human head. A heavy jaw, teeth bared into something far more threatening than a smile, a flattish nose, a low forehead masked by a mop of straggly hair, and a thick brow-ridge that shields two bloodshot eyes: the face of an animal, but an animal with a new intelligence.

Now *ergaster* stops still, comfortable with his distance from the ailing wildebeest, which, exhausted, collapses resignedly into the mud. The hunter's eyes focus on it attentively. The hair on his head is greying, marking him out clearly as an older individual. Beside him are other similar hominids; together they make up a small party devoted to gathering food. They all stand in silence, watching the weakening wildebeest.

For *ergaster*, feeding is rooted in opportunism and patience. They do not have the speed to be pursuit predators, or the strength to ambush large prey. Typically, they scavenge whatever meat they can find that has been left over from a big-cat kill, and as a troop they are more than able to see off any vultures that may have congregated by a carcass. But when opportunity presents itself, they will themselves take an old or ailing creature. Their method is slow but effective: their bodies have evolved the limbs and stamina to walk and stalk their quarry into the ground. Searching for meat can last a day or more, but the rewards are great.

The older male stands, impassive, watching the prey. It is obvious that he is judging the moment to move closer. An older female stands near him. Clearly past childbearing age, she too can help with the slow and steady hunt. Beside them a younger male appears more on edge, eyes darting from view to view. A successful kill is a rare event, and he is excited. Suddenly and without prompting he takes off, running past the older male and the rest of the group. A second young male follows him, and the two rush towards the

Perhaps surprisingly an older female would have been part of a scavenging party.

(ABOVE) The impatient young *ergaster* male does not wait for the signal to attack the prey.

(OPPOSITE) The old *ergaster* has learned many skills for stalking and scavenging, and knows that a trophy, like the crocodile tooth he holds in his mouth, marks him out as special.

wildebeest, brandishing wooden stabbing implements. The two hunters scream and yell, disturbing the quiet of the landscape as they bear down on the prostrate animal in front of them, confident of their attack. But gradually their calls fall away as the mud around the waterhole starts to slow them down. Then, extraordinarily, there is a twitch of life from the wildebeest. Roused to a final effort, it takes a huge breath and, as the two hunters continue to struggle through the mud towards it, it rises to its feet and staggers on. Suddenly it finds firmer ground and, with a last gasp, it is free and on its way to join the rest of the herd.

The opportunity for a kill is lost. The young male and his friend know they have made fools of themselves and, as they extract themselves from the mud and dust and slope back towards the group, the old female gesticulates, and barks strange nasal sounds at them. If she had words to describe her feelings, she would call them impatient fools, but her concept of language is not that subtle. For the old male, however, their spontaneous interruption of his killing technique has passed without effect. He still clearly knows best, and is still dominant. Impassively, he turns towards the direction of the wildebeest herd, scratching his face with a long crocodile tooth that he has been holding. It is trophy of a previous encounter, and he has learned that he is seen as being special for having gained it. His knowledge of the animals they hunt, the techniques he uses, the skills of the kill, they have all taken many years to perfect, and his wisdom still counts. Meanwhile, there is that wildebeest to catch. The relentless stalking begins again.

MIDDAY HUNTER

The key to *ergaster*'s survival is a set of remarkable evolutionary adaptations to the environment into which it emerged. For the two to three million years after upright walking began among the earliest human ancestors, the world had been going through a relentless phase of gradual cooling and, as the ice caps at the poles steadily locked up more and more water in their frozen masses, so the world became drier too. By two million years ago, the dominant environment in

Secrets of the skeleton

'Let's just go as far as that little tree, and if we don't find anything more, we'll call it quits.' With that sentiment, the scientist Richard Leakey agreed with his colleague Alan Walker that there was a limit to how much fossil-hunting could be done when there was little chance of success. In the summer of 1984 Leakey and Walker were leading a dig for fossils on the west side of Lake Turkana in northern Kenya, and a few days earlier their lead fossil-finder, Kamoya Kimeu, a Kenyan with an extraordinary knack for spotting hominid remains in parched ground, had come across a tiny fragment of the skull of a *Homo erectus* (now renamed as *Homo ergaster*) at a new site. Over the next days more fragments were unearthed, including some ribs, which are very rarely found in fossil mammals because they are either the first to be consumed by the scavengers of the dead body, or they are crushed by the sediments over the millennia of fossilization.

But no more substantial pieces had come out of the ground, and as the two men approached the acacia tree they were actually looking forward to striking camp and moving on to more promising locations. And then, there, with the tree root literally growing through it, they came upon the rest of the skull – the acacia tree had seeded itself inside the upturned braincase. Over the next month what emerged from the soil by Lake Turkana was perhaps the most spectacular set of hominid remains ever

found: skull, jaw, neck, spine, shoulders, arms, ribs pelvis, thighs and legs – the skeleton was 40 per cent complete; the only substantial parts missing were the feet and hands.

From the start, the skeleton began to reveal remarkable details of the living creature it had once been. The pelvis was male, the jaw had no sockets for wisdom teeth, and the sutures, or joints, in the skull bones had not fused together, so he was an adolescent boy. He became known as Nariokotome Boy, named after the site itself. He had died one and a half million years ago. The pattern of development and wear of his teeth suggested he had lived to the age of about ten years, although the skeleton seems as developed as a fourteen-year-old of today, suggesting that *ergaster* would have reached full maturity much earlier than we do, around fifteen years. The size of his bones indicated that he had weighed 35 kilograms (5 stone) and was 160 centimetres (5 feet 3 inches) tall, so as an adult he would have been a striking 190 centimetres (6 feet) tall, and 69 kilograms (nearly 11 stone): an impressive size.

The tall body shape, with its similarities to the modern-day Masai people of East Africa, gave clues to how the creature lost heat in the tropical sun – through sweating from the large area of smooth skin of its body, rather than panting. The skull revealed that it would have had the beginnings of a nose. This allowed more efficient cooling, via the

air breathed in and out, and ensured that every drop of moisture in the air was retained as it left the body. This new adaptation to a hot climate suggested that *ergaster* was far more active than its ancestors – which also fits with the tall, lanky skeleton. He was a potential runner, and the structure of his hips suggests he was a very good one, for they are much narrower than ours, and the joint with his thighs is far more efficiently constructed.

Throughout life, bones constantly reshape themselves according to the amount of stress and strain placed on them by activity. The application of engineering beam theory to the cross-sectional structure of Nariokotome Boy's bones revealed that he was exceptionally strong compared to modern humans, suggesting a very tough and active life. Also, his right forearm and shoulder were slightly larger than the left, and the brain-case of the skull revealed that one side of his brain was larger than the other: he was a right-hander.

The narrowness of *ergaster*'s hips may have been highly efficient for running and walking, but it meant that babies were born while their brain was still developing, or the skull would have been too big to pass through the birth canal. This is where the long period of infant dependency probably first evolved (see the feature on pages 84–5). So *ergaster* society had to be geared around care for the children over a period of years. The size of the group needed to be large, and the web of relationships between its members needed to be strong.

One other very special fossil find reveals just how strong the bonds were. Ten years earlier, Kamoya had found another partially complete skeleton of a female *ergaster,* but the bones were distorted and their shape obscured because by chance the individual had died of a serious bone disease. It turned out to be 'hypervitaminosis', an excess of vitamin A, which is stored up in the liver. It can be contracted from eating too much of the livers of carnivorous animals, which have themselves eaten many livers, and so built up a great residue of toxins. So the death of this individual *ergaster* immediately confirmed the intensely carnivorous nature of the species, but it also revealed a clue to their society. For this female had suffered for a long period of time. The disease was so advanced that she must have been immobile and in agony for weeks before she died. So the others in the group must have looked after her. They cared for their sick.

The cause of death of individual fossil creatures is very rarely found, but in the case of Nariokotome Boy the condition of the skull revealed the poignant details of his final moments. In his lower jaw, one of his adult premolar teeth had just begun to push through, but the milk-tooth that it replaced had broken away, leaving behind two tiny pieces of root canal, exposed to the surface of his gum. Perhaps he had impatiently pulled at the tooth instead

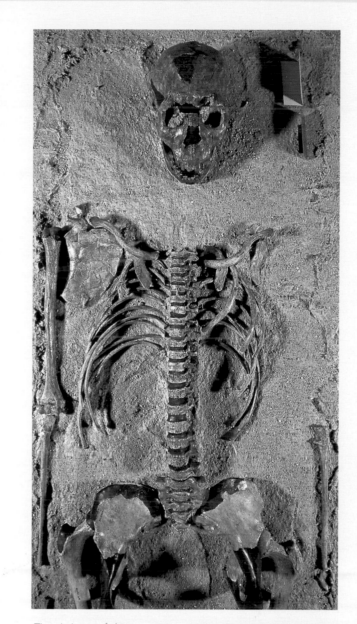

The skeleton of the young *ergaster* boy found at Nariokotome revealed striking similarities with the body of a modern human.

of waiting for it to fall out. The exposed root canal became infected, and an abscess formed that became so severe that it left its mark on the jawbone itself – a clue to the septicaemia that must have

overwhelmed his body as a result. He fell face down and died in the sediment of a muddy pool, which quickly preserved his remains, along with the footprints of a hippo that had trodden over his lifeless body.

An elderly female *ergaster*.

East Africa was open, dry savannah, a precursor to the vast familiar grasslands of places like the Serengeti. As the hominids began to colonize this landscape, so the evolutionary pressure on them produced physical changes that have become the hallmarks of all human beings. And the driver of this change was the sun.

At noon on the early savannah the temperature can be 35°C (95°F) in the shade – but here on the flat there is no shade. The *ergaster* are the only hunters around at this hour. The big cats, and even the hyenas, lie panting and dozing while the sun is at its height, but these hominids can seize this hunting opportunity from the competition. Just as today, when different human beings who have developed in different climates show features that are adaptations to their world, so it is for the early hominids. Today, the Inuit people of the Arctic have adapted to their cold climate to arrive at a short, squat body shape, because this minimizes the surface area of skin exposed to the air, and so retains the maximum amount of the body's warmth. On the other hand, the Masai people of East Africa are tall and very thin, maximizing the surface area of the body from which to lose heat, and at the same time keeping the area of body directly exposed to the sun overhead to a minimum – just the head and shoulders. The tall thin skeleton of *ergaster* is just such a response to the hot climate of two million years ago, and has evolved over hundreds of thousands of years to form this new heat-efficient species.

But *ergaster*'s evolutionary fitness does not end with the long tall frame. Its thin upright physique means that no longer does it need a fur covering on its body to protect areas directly exposed to the sun. Instead, it has a large area of smooth skin, and that enables it to lose heat by a newly evolved, but highly effective mechanism. *Ergaster* cools down by sweating, far more efficient than the panting used by other, fur-covered animals. And it has another new, but familiar, human feature. It is the first hominid to have a nose: not quite the wide beak of the later Neanderthals, or the protruding feature of modern humans, but a real nose nonetheless. All previous hominid ancestors had nostrils that lay sunken into the surface of the face, but *ergaster*'s nose sticks out, allowing more air to be cooled and moistened by the lining of the nostrils before reaching the lungs, and at the same time allowing more moisture to be retained in the body on breathing out. The newly evolved sweat glands and nose give *ergaster* the edge in the hot African day. Their lanky skeleton provides long powerful limbs, very strong, and ideally suited to running, while their new efficient heat management means they can run, walk, and keep walking for a long period of time.

THE NEW BRAIN

The troop of hominids walks steadily on, untiring, while in the far distance the image of a herd of moving animals ripples in and out of focus through the heat-haze. It is impossible to see exactly what they are. The older man pauses and looks down at a series of regular marks on the ground. They are hoof-prints and, tracing one with his finger, he looks from them to the distant herd, making the connection – they must be giraffes. It may seem a simple act of observation to us, but in that single moment, *ergaster* reveals the secret of what really marks him out as a different kind of species. It is not the remarkably human-like body, but the thing that resides inside that un-human head. For, at a volume of about 1,000 cubic centimetres (60 cubic inches), *ergaster*'s brain is half as big again as the smartest of his predecessors, and almost within the limits of modern human variation. (No one person has exactly the same sized brain as another, and some have significantly smaller brains than others, with no great distinction in intelligence or ability.) This new brain capacity has brought even greater powers of thought into the everyday life of our ancestor.

Homo ergaster learned to read tracks and signs left by animals.

127

He holds a beautifully symmetrical, teardrop-shaped stone hand-axe

All animals have some understanding of their environments. A five-month old swallow is instinctively able to negotiate the 10,000-kilometre (6,000-mile) migration from Britain to southern Africa without ever having done the journey before. An old matriarch elephant can remember where, in her vast territory, to go for water at a certain time of year. Earlier hominids such as *habilis* and *rudolfensis* had already learned to associate different signs in their environment, such as the wheeling of vultures in the sky as a sign of a kill. But *ergaster* has taken that further, making complex deductions about apparently unrelated events going on around them. They can look at marks in the sand and, never having seen them before, can tell at once what they are, and what they are likely to relate to. To a dog, a big cat, or even to a baboon, hoof-marks such as these are no more than just that: random marks. Only we, of all the animals on Earth today, can see them for what they are: hoof-prints, made by an animal that is likely either to be a meal for us or to make a meal of us. *Ergaster* is very likely the creature that we inherited that skill from.

Silently, the old male turns away and leads the party on. Now he can make sense of the blurry movement shimmering in the distance, he knows it is of no interest to him. He knows his quarry, and he is gaining on it. But the younger male stands a little way apart from the group, looking at some other markings. He too is trying to learn to make links. Suddenly the older male barks at him, clearly angry that this distraction is slowing them down. He does not want his kill to be spoilt for a second time.

Ergaster's improved ability to make deductions about the world they live in, and apply them to totally unfamiliar things around them, has given them much greater adaptability than the earlier hominids. It is a milestone on the journey that will lead modern humans to being able not just to understand our environment but to actually control it.

Once again the hunting party has come to a stop. Clutched in the old *ergaster*'s hand is the tangible proof of his abilities. At some time in the last half million years, he and his kind have made a remarkable technological breakthrough. He holds a beautifully symmetrical, teardrop-shaped stone hand-axe, and its bevelled edges glint with beauty and menace in the bright African sun. It is a stone object that is the product of a thoughtful mind – a mind that could identify an ideal nodule of stone, could hold a plan of how to turn it into a knife, could carefully select the point at which to strike it with another rock, and then consistently work the flakes as they break away, gradually refining the stone, first one side then the other, to a razor-sharp, elegantly symmetrical blade. Powerful and adaptable as a tool, it can even be touched up or sharpened; the creation of this hand-axe shows planning and vision. They are known today as 'Acheulean' axes, and they are of an order of sophistication greater than that of the bi-facial choppers made by *habilis* and his kind. They clearly reveal that their makers were intelligent and highly skilled, and – because examples are found all

Homo ergaster made a major step forward in the working of stone tools, creating symmetrical hand-axes.

A mind set in stone

A major hurdle to understanding how the thinking of our earliest ancestors evolved is that thoughts and feelings do not fossilize. However, the artefacts that they left behind do provide some clues. For about two million years, these consisted only of stone tools, but by studying how they were made a surprising amount can be deduced about the early human mind.

The first stone tools, which appeared at the time of *Homo habilis,* are called Oldowan, after the site at Olduvai in Tanzania where they were first found. Although they are not very beautiful items, they are the product of considerable skill. Producing flakes by stone-knapping is no simple matter. In order to produce flakes as a matter of course, a toolmaker needs to select the right kind of core, one with an edge that is angled quite sharply (less than ninety degrees) so that when struck by the hammerstone it produces a single sharp flake rather than shattering into several pieces. The toolmaker also has to strike the stone in exactly the right place, about one centimetre (barely half an inch) from the edge, and with an angled, glancing blow. An analysis of the cores and flakes from hominid sites shows that the toolmakers of two and a half million years ago had fully mastered the skill of stone-knapping, producing them regularly and with ease, and were not merely hammering away at random in the hope of producing flakes by a lucky fluke.

For a million years after their appearance there was no appreciable change in the nature of the stone tools. However, in Africa, around one and a half million years ago, Homo *ergaster* seems to have made a dramatic change in the nature of stone tools. There is no obvious reason why but suddenly much more refined, teardrop-shaped hand-axes appear in the fossil record. These are known as Acheulean tools (after the place in France where they were first found, although dating from a much later period). They display clear symmetry, with the toolmaker now carefully shaping the core piece of stone, rather than simply focusing on getting the sharp edge.

First, a suitable piece of stone must be selected, and a hard hammerstone is used to get the basic shape by striking flakes off it from alternate sides. Then thinner and thinner flakes are struck off, working round the tool; much later archaeological sites reveal that bone or wooden hammers were used to remove these ever-thinner flakes. Both the sharpened core and any useful flakes were used for a variety of different purposes, from hacking to slicing and scraping. Clearly the *ergaster* who made them had a mental map at the outset, and worked the stone to fit it, adapting their technique for the shape of each individual stone nodule that they started with.

The first Europeans, *Homo heidelbergensis,* around 500,000 years ago, were still using the Acheulean method, although by then it is clear that the tools were being made systematically, in what may be described as workshops, where hundreds of flaked tools have been found together. The tools reveal a clear skill, anticipation, judgement, and even an appreciation of visual balance, but it is interesting that the hominids who made them display no other expression of creativity in their lives. So what was going on in their minds as they sat there knapping?

The archaeologist Steven Mithen argues that they had different kinds of intelligence. They had a technical intelligence for their toolmaking, they had natural history intelligence for their environment, and they had some social intelligence for dealing with their fellow beings. But these three did not really overlap in any kind of sophisticated general intelligence such as we have. It is hard to imagine such restricted thinking, but an experience that we all share may give a clue. Many of us have experienced driving a car and suddenly realizing that we have travelled for some distance, and surely encountered many moments where we had to think, make careful judgements and act, but we have absolutely no recollection of having done so. This has been described as a kind of 'rolling consciousness' with a very short-term memory. At the time of driving we are thinking about the problems, but later it is all gone.

Perhaps that gives an insight into how the early humans lived their lives. They could think effectively about the here and now, but little else beyond.

Another sea change in the hominid tool-kit comes at around 250,000 years ago. It is widely seen among the Neanderthals, in the form of the Levallois method of knapping. Here the aim is to remove a very precisely shaped flake from the core of a nodule. That flake then becomes a fine point, perhaps to be used as the tip of a stabbing spear. The great advantage was that each such flake had a long, continuous and razor-sharp cutting edge, rather than the chipped edge produced by repeatedly working at the edge of a core. The technique requires the knapping of the core into a convex shape, from which the final pointed flake is removed; this usually requires no further refinement before it is used. The Neanderthals were able to strike many such useful flakes off the stone, and then restore the convex shape they had first created, and strike off several more points. It is an extraordinary skill, requiring careful sophisticated mental processes, and it is reckoned that no one today can match their remarkable ability – but it was a very narrow ability.

Only with the emergence of the modern humans, *Homo sapiens,* comes a diversity of toolmaking that reveals connections being made across different parts of the mind. Called Aurignacian (after Aurignac, in France), the tools that appear 40,000 years ago are of a different order altogether. Now the toolmaker was producing different kinds of blade from a single stone core –

The progression of stone tool-making by our ancestors. An Oldowan pebble tool (left), an Acheulean blade from East Africa (middle) and a Levallois flake found at Swanley in Kent (right).

scrapers, knives, spearpoints, engraving tools or piercers – clearly a far more advanced mental map was at work. But also other materials began to be used: bone, antler, ivory, wood and twine. This reveals how the modern humans were drawing knowledge from every aspect of their world, and applying it practically, to make hooks, needles, harpoons and rope.

Creativity had arrived. And with it came incredible efficiency. Whereas at the dawn of the age of stone tools, a half-kilo (one-pound) lump of flint would have provided about 50 milimetres (2 inches) of cutting edge, by the height of the stone age in Europe a Cro-Magnon toolmaker could get up to ten metres (over thirty feet) of cutting surface from the same lump: hundreds of tiny flakes, each with a lethal edge.

(ABOVE) The scavenging party patiently awaits the moment to strike.

(OPPOSITE) The scavenging party of *ergaster* immediately eat their fill of the wildebeest.

over Africa – that they were in a society that passed on skills from one person to another. Right now, a million and a half years before our time, it is the most complicated thing ever made on the planet.

The older male is trying to see track marks on the ground, but without success, and his anxiety is beginning to show. Meanwhile the younger male is again becoming distracted – he is using his own hand-axe to lever some bark away from a dried-up bush. Suddenly there is a flurry. The wildebeest is spotted, again on the ground. The moment has arrived. The young male trots up to the rest of the group again, and they all stand, tense and expectant, awaiting the command. But this time there is no dissent, or premature action. The older male waits to be certain the beast is really labouring again. Then it is happening. He makes a barely perceptible signal. This is a process they have been through before and, once launched at the stricken animal, they will make a formidable team of killers. Not crying out this time, they simply run, their long legs moving almost effortlessly as they bear down on their prey, and the wildebeest has neither energy nor time to escape. As they reach it, the first hand-axe thuds down into the animal's neck; then a second. There is no real defence, and the creature is soon dead.

But here the distinction between ourselves and *ergaster* is starkly drawn. The small group immediately begin to satisfy their hunger on the carcass: tearing at the flesh and sinews with their powerful jaws and teeth, slashing more skin from the animal's body with their sharp axes, lifting their heads only briefly and sharply to watch and listen for approaching predators, before bending again to the feast. Out on the baking mudflat a fast, silent and bloody meal is being taken.

Fossil remains of *ergaster* have revealed teeth worn away in a pattern that could be caused only by a lot of chewing at flesh.

At the time these creatures are living, a million years have passed since meat became part of the food of the hominid line. Fossil remains of *ergaster* have revealed teeth worn away in a pattern that could be caused only by a lot of chewing at flesh. For *ergaster*, the reliance on meat has become key, and in this remarkable species it is possible to see the great evolutionary benefit of that shift in diet. As a source of nourishment, meat is about a hundred times more energy-efficient than any vegetarian combination; a herbivorous animal has to eat about a hundred times the weight of plants compared to the weight of meat that would provide the same amount of energy to a carnivore. So the size of gut needed to process food is far greater for a herbivore than a carnivore. The complex stomachs and intestines that ruminant animals have evolved are so big that much of the energy they get from their food is used up simply in processing it. For *ergaster*, its slim skeleton reveals how much smaller its stomach is than that of any hominid that came before. Instead of a rib-cage that widens out as it goes down, to encompass a huge plant-eating gut, as in chimpanzees, or the other early hominids, the *ergaster* rib-cage remains slender at the bottom, allowing for a small stomach, just like that of modern humans. A small stomach means that not much energy is being consumed in processing food, so *ergaster*'s food energy is available to be spent on something else: for there is one other organ in the body that requires vast amounts of energy, far more than even the gut: it is the brain.

Running the brain is the most energy-intense process in any animal. For example, brain tissue has twenty-two times the rate of metabolism of muscle, so you need twenty-two times more energy to think than to walk about. In fact the modern human brain uses up a fifth of all the calories that we take in each day, even though it

Homo ergaster

Who discovered *ergaster*?

The first fossil of *Homo ergaster* ('work-man') was a cranium, complete with eye sockets, nose and face, discovered in 1975 at Koobi Fora in northern Kenya. It was found by Bernard Ngeneo, a Kenyan working in Richard Leakey's team, which was known as the 'Hominid Gang' of fossil finders. The most complete specimen is the one known as Nariokotome Boy, found in 1984 (see the feature on pages 124–5), and it is also one of the most spectacular fossil discoveries ever made, with 40 per cent of the entire skeleton of a single individual having been found. At first these fossils were regarded as an African *Homo erectus* (Upright Man, a species discovered in Java in 1891), but more recently they have been reclassified as *ergaster*, with *erectus* now only being used to describe the Asian descendants.

When did *ergaster* live?

Ergaster first appeared around 1.9 million years ago. This was a time when the robust australopithecines were still in existence, and so its discovery immediately upset the notion that there had been a single line of descent from our earliest ancestors to the present day. Here were more than one species co-existing. But *ergaster* and *erectus* were the longest surviving hominid species ever to have walked the planet. In Africa, *ergaster* died out about 600,000 years ago, but *erectus* lived on in Asia until less than 50,000 years before today.

Where did *ergaster* live?

Fossil remains of *ergaster* or *erectus* have been discovered in eastern and southern Africa, Georgia in the Caucasus, Indonesia (Java) and in China. It was the first hominid species to migrate out of Africa, and it spread throughout the Middle East and Asia, and into eastern Europe. Its descendants are thought to have been the first hominids to enter western Europe. Its remarkable ability to live in a wide variety of environments shows that it had a new intelligence that enabled it to be very adaptable, and to survive in new and unfamiliar landscapes.

What did *ergaster* look like?

The Nariokotome Boy skeleton revealed that *ergaster* had evolved dramatically away from the ape-like shape of its ancestors. Its body was very similar to our own: long-limbed, upright, slim-hipped, narrow-waisted with a small stomach and a chest shaped very like ours – not the barrel shape of the apes. A male would have weighed about 66 kilograms (10 stone), and he was very tall, at 180 centimetres (nearly 6 feet). They were well adapted to the heat of East Africa, in the same way that modern Masai people are. He would have had virtually no body hair, with smooth, olive-coloured skin. His face sported what could be called the first nose in the human fossil record. His brain was large; two-thirds the size of ours. It is likely that it was the first hominid to have developed the whites of the eyes.

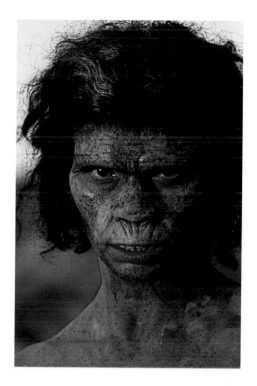

Female *Homo ergaster*.

How would *ergaster* have lived?

Ergaster would have eaten pretty much anything, and were principally foragers of roots, fruit, berries, birds' eggs and so on. But they were also scavengers of meat, which now played an important part in their regular diet, as it provided a supply of extra energy, needed for the larger brain. Their large brains also allowed them to manage more complex social structure than their ancestors. For the first time males and females would have formed pair-bondings for a period of time, as the males began to invest in the rearing of their offspring, and the females could rely on support through a long period of infant care. Food would have been brought back from scavenging or killing, in order to share it with another individual who was of value: a partner, or a potential mate.

135

The old male *ergaster* uses his whole body to carry a 'vest' of meat.

makes up only 2 per cent of our body weight. It is not possible for any creature to have a large gut and a large brain – there just is not enough energy in the body to go round. Our brain is nearly five times larger than would be expected of a mammal of our body size, while our gut is only half as big. So it is fortunate for *ergaster*, and indeed for us, that their ancestors began the shift to meat, because without that simple act the hominid brain could never have evolved to the size it has reached.

But within all those statistics there lies a puzzle: what was it that drove the evolution of the larger brain? What made the hominid brain such an advantage to have that it was worth devoting so much energy to it?

THE FIRST BUTCHERS

The gorging on the mudflat is drawing to a close. The hunting party has eaten its fill of the soft fleshy meat, and sinews and skin lie torn and sliced around the carcass. The stone tools are bloodied and worn from the crush against bone. But the *ergaster* are not yet finished with their kill. Calmly, the older male begins to flake the edge of his hand-axe with another stone, sharpening the edge, before bringing it down with great force on to a limb joint. Now the blade is brought across the animal's hide with a new brutal skill – butchery. Gradually the other hominids begin to do the same, and steadily the remains of the wildebeest are dismembered.

Some way off, a single lion has begun to approach the kill. The *ergaster* work quickly, edgily glancing around them for signs of trouble from the interloper. They know what a lion can do, but also the lion has learnt that a troop of these hominids is not something to take on lightly. They are scavengers that he cannot simply chase away with a show of raw aggression. These creatures are clever enough to fight him back, as a team, and so he waits till they have completed their work. And it does not take them long. Within a few minutes there are hocks of meat lying ready, the older male has slung a 'vest' of meaty skin around his neck, and there are chunks of bone being heaved onto shoulders, as the party begins to set off on the long walk back from their kill.

Steadily the remains of the wildebeest are dismembered.

Ergaster's big brains have provided them with useful new skills and new technology, and have changed the way they view their world. But, strangely, none of these would seem to have demanded that the brain evolve to be so large. Scavenging in groups has been perfected in many other creatures, and although the new stone hand-axes require substantial intelligence to make, fossil discoveries have revealed that *ergaster*'s large brain was already in existence half a million years before the new tools were invented. Instead, the clue to the large brain lies in what they do with the meat they have gathered. *Ergaster* are the first hominids to have developed the skill of disjointing a carcass in order to take the meat away to share. They have learned that there are advantages to giving what is left to particular individuals – they get something in return. *Ergaster* have the most complex social relationships of any creature to have walked the Earth by this time. As a result, they need every bit of brain power that they can bring to bear.

(BELOW) Both sexes would have had smooth skin, and the faintest covering of body hair.

(OVERLEAF) The *ergaster* troop return from the kill.

FRIENDS AND FAMILY

Far from the hunting party, away from the baking mudflat, nestled amid some grassy dunes, lies a small area of wet ground with shrubs and trees – an oasis in the dry East African landscape,

and a place where the main group of *ergaster* are gathered. To call it a 'camp' is too sophisticated a word. These are creatures for whom movement is the norm, and here they are gathered to rest, recover from exertions, care for a sick or old member of the group, and await the scavengers' return.

It is a busy scene. There are around twenty individuals in this group, but mostly here are the females and the youngsters. An *ergaster* will not be fully mature until it is twelve to fifteen years old, and during their long upbringing the children must learn quickly about the world around them, or have little chance of survival. In the dunes and scrub around the watering place, the females and children have been foraging for additional food: anything from the large African insects to birds' eggs, fruits, berries and occasional roots. For although meat is a primary source of energy, *ergaster* will eat almost anything.

(OPPOSITE) Although meat was an important part of the *ergaster* diet, they relied heavily on gathering fruits and any other available food.

(ABOVE) The successful return of the scavenging party prompts much excitement in the whole group.

Songs and words

The origins of language and speech have long been debated among scientists, and there is no current agreement on when or why they emerged. But one theory highlights intriguing clues to the first utterances of the early hominids. In modern humans, singing in chorus has the ability to touch our deepest, primitive emotions; bodies sway together in harmony, feet stomp, and an almost hypnotic effect comes over us. Look at other primates and 'singing' can be found in many species: for example, the contact calls of gelada baboons and the pant-hooting of chimpanzees build up in a chorus that can whip up the troop and get them all synchronized in the same emotional state of excitement. They begin drumming, stomping and branch-waving at the same time. It suggests that singing evolved from a deep ancestral past, and is therefore a fundamental basis for the emergence of primitive language.

One of the most prominent differences between hominid and other primate singing is that humans have evolved an ability to maintain a sustained steady rhythm, like a pulse or beat. The advantage of this may well be that the steady beat enables a much larger group of creatures to join in the vocalizing, so that the 'song' becomes well co-ordinated, which would be a much more effective and off-putting display to any potential attacker than the cacophony of random frightened voices.

The size of the hominid groups is also a clue to the origin of language. There is a very simple piece of scientific research showing that the size of a primate's brain is directly correlated with the size of the group of animals that it operates within, immediately or in a wider context. For example, tiny-brained gibbons live in tightly bound groups of just four to six, while chimps, with their larger brains, live in groups of fifty or so. Modern humans feel most comfortable living among groups of about 150, which is a figure found consistently across the world, in hunter–gatherer societies, and also in the remains of whole Neolithic villages that have been uncovered. The significance of such a group size has turned out to be important for the emergence of language.

To maintain relationships in a group, it is necessary to socialize. Chimps and other primates do this by extensive grooming. They can spend hours simply sitting and picking parasites out of the hair of another individual, forming an intimate bond with the other chimp – call it friendship, perhaps – as they do so. But the larger the social group, the more time has to be spent grooming, and there is a limit. In fact no primates are able to spend more than 20 per cent of their daily time on social bonding, as they have other necessary activities – feeding, travelling and rest – to undertake too, if they are to survive. If social bonding is done by

Primates spend up to 20 per cent of their time grooming others in their group.

physically grooming their way around all the other primates in their group, then a limit of about seventy individuals is about as many as time will allow them to deal with. For modern humans to build relationships with up to 150, something else has taken over from grooming. The argument is that language is that something.

Our ability to communicate thoughts and feelings to others has enabled our living groups to get larger, and thus stronger, and safer. The size of *Homo ergaster*'s brain suggests that they were comfortable with relationships with about 110 other individuals, so *ergaster* almost certainly marks the moment in our evolution when basic calls of alarm and courtship gave way to primitive conversation.

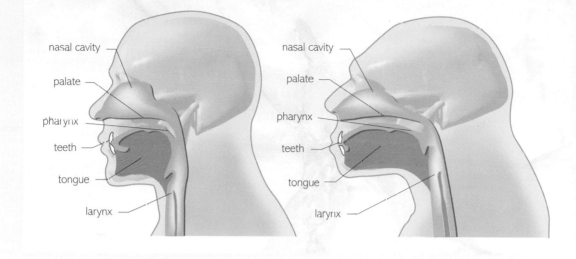

Vocal tract of a modern human (left) and a Neanderthal (right).

The physical equipment needed to create speech is straightforward: the larynx, which is the structure in the neck that contains the vocal cords; the pharynx, which is a tube that runs up from the larynx and opens out into the mouth and nasal cavity; and the tongue. Speech occurs when air rises from the lungs and passes over the vocal cords, which vibrate to make a sound. This is then modified by the muscles that squeeze and change the shape of the pharynx as the air passes through. Most articulation of speech occurs in the pharynx, with the tongue providing the final precise expression of the sound.

In all other primates, even our closest relative the chimpanzee, the larynx is high in the throat and thus the pharynx is too short to achieve any complex modification of sound. In humans the larynx is much lower in the neck, creating a long pharynx.

The fossil record shows that in *Homo ergaster*, who lived from 1.9 million years ago, the descent of the larynx was under way, possibly due to the changes in breathing that came from the tall upright body, but also in order to allow for correct swallowing in the newly evolved relationship between the jaw and the skull. It was likely to have been able to make many of the sounds of speech, but not all. *Homo heidelbergensis* who lived around 500,000 years ago, had an almost modern vocal tract, and thus nearly a full range of human sounds. But their speech would have sounded different from ours due to differences in the shape of the nose and the size of the face. The speaking abilities of the Neanderthals who lived from 250,000 years ago, is a hotly disputed area of research. But the discovery of a fossilized hyoid bone (which supports the larynx) in a Neanderthal skeleton at the Kebara cave in Israel reveals it to be virtually identical to that of a human, suggesting they had an effectively modern vocal tract. Certainly, the Neanderthals' large brain size, as well as other evidence of their behaviour, suggests they must have had quite considerable communication skills.

The emergence of fully modern language and speech, however, came only with anatomically modern humans. But here again, there is much debate as to when and where that occurred. It all hangs on our ancestors' first use of symbolism and imaginative thinking. Some argue that this did not occur until 40,000 years ago, with the dramatic 'explosion' of creativity that we see in the magnificent cave paintings in Europe. However, there are clear signs of imagination and creativity in the *Homo sapiens* that emerged in Africa up to 100,000 years ago, in the form of carved bone tools, patterns etched on stone, and the use of red ochre colouring. So it is likely that the need to express complex abstract ideas in language had evolved by then.

143

There is an atmosphere of friendship between the creatures

The older female offers food to her pregnant daughter. *Ergaster* developed the beginnings of relationships based on sharing and helping each other.

It is the foraging group who hear the returning party first. It is not the sound of their tread nearby that gives them away, but instead they are heard from much further away. The scavengers no longer need to keep the silence of the chase. Instead they are free to enjoy the success of their kill, and to trumpet the news to others in the group. The sound that the foragers can hear can only be described as singing. The loud calls of alarm and bonding that all primate groups display evolved very early in our ancestral line, and 'singing' is a common feature in the primate world. But the tall *ergaster* body has conferred a new ability on to these hominids. By losing heat through their newly evolved sweat glands under the skin, *ergaster* has freed the lungs and airways from the requirement of constant panting in the hot climate. Freed from this constraint, the lungs and diaphragm have evolved to provide a more controlled airflow through the throat and mouth. The result is a new kind of control over the sounds that they emit, and in *ergaster* the rudiments of primitive speech almost certainly have made their first appearance in human evolution.

The faint rhythmic sound is becoming louder in the stillness of the hot evening. Some of the waiting hominids have stood up, and begin to walk towards the echo of the returning scavengers. Suddenly they are seen, emerging over the rise of a dune. All have returned, and they are laden with meat. An immediate buzz of excitement runs through the group, and we now see an intricate web of relationships unfold, revealing the full complexity of the *ergaster* social life.

There is an atmosphere of friendship between the creatures, as the hunters show off their booty, and the youngsters flock to the source of food. But the party quickly breaks up as the scavengers pair up with other individuals, and move off to separate parts of the oasis to feed. The old female seeks out another younger female in the camp who is clearly expecting a child. They greet each other and the older one hands over some food; they are mother and daughter, and briefly they eat together, before the older female moves off. The older male strides up to the pregnant female, clearly the father of the unborn child, and gives her some meat. She greets him with affection, and the two sit and groom each other as they eat, she occasionally scratching caked mud from his limbs, he picking dried blood from her face.

Sharing meat from the kill has increased the young male's chance of finding the mate he wants.

Ergaster society marks the beginning of a kind of relationship that has become crucial to human existence: the pairing up of males and females in partnerships. The evolution of the larger brain, alongside the narrower pelvis that comes with upright walking, has meant that infants are now born before their brains have fully developed. *Ergaster* children therefore have a very long period of infant dependency while the brain continues to grow, and while they learn the many complex things that are involved in *ergaster* society. As a result, the energy demands now placed on a female while rearing her young are huge, so there are tremendous mutual advantages to forming a bond with a partner. Females know there is someone to supplement their foraging diet with high-quality meat, and also help protect their children, who now have such a long period of infancy. In return, males can know for

the beginnings of language have emerged, with their rudimentary speech enabling *ergaster* to form relationships

certain whether or not a female's offspring is really theirs, and so it is worth investing their time in support for the child.

This is perhaps a scene unlike any other seen on Earth up to this time. It is a group of animals held together not just by safety in numbers, and not by the domination of a single all-powerful male, but by something more collaborative and potentially much more powerful: by the ties of family, and friends. Co-operation – helping others, and relying on others to help you – has become a powerful force that holds the group together. Underpinning *ergaster*'s social system is a newly emerging idea: trust. They are dependent on being able to understand motives and being able to know that both sides of a bargain will be held to.

Managing this complex world of *ergaster* relationships is the key to what has driven the evolution of their brain. The size of the full *ergaster* group is probably a little over a hundred individuals – usually broken up into smaller foraging groups like this one, with the full number coming together in times of plenty, when they would need to interact well together. This is a far larger and more complex group than was maintained by any of their ancestors. But along with the bigger brains needed simply to track those other individuals, the consequence of such a large network of relationships has been to kick-start another peculiarly human attribute. In order to bond with the other members of the group, the *ergaster* no longer totally rely on physically grooming them in the way that the earlier hominids did. There are simply too many individuals for them to have the time to do that. Instead, the beginnings of language have emerged, with their rudimentary speech enabling *ergaster* to form relationships and maintain them across a much wider group. Thus their upright physique, their larger brains and their more complex groups have come together to produce this most significant evolutionary step.

(OPPOSITE) *Ergaster* marked the beginning of forming male–female partnerships in hominids, with each gaining an advantage for the upbringing of their young.

146

LOVE AND RIVALRY

The impetuous younger male hunter swaggers around the group, posturing, standing upright, eager to be noticed by the others. For him, the kill and his role in it have been particularly important. It means he has not returned empty-handed, and will have some meat with which to woo the young female that he wants to mate with. She, meanwhile, is sitting beneath a tree at the edge of the group, eating berries, with juices running down her chin and chest. There are other younger females nearby, and she seems oblivious at first to the fact that she is the focus of any attention. She smiles as the younger male walks over to her and hands her some meat, and they begin to talk.

There will never be any knowing what kind of rudimentary words these creatures might have been able to use. Certainly their language would go beyond purely emotional knee-jerk calls. They probably had words or sounds that were names for each other, words for feelings of happy or sad or fear, and words that would cover concepts to do with people. Perhaps, they would have had a word for 'friend'. They may even have been able to string emotions and thoughts together. But they would have had no comprehension of syntax or grammar or tenses, just a simple combination of words that would make sense according to the circumstances. So 'Happy meat' might mean 'I'm pleased that the hunt was successful', and 'Happy meat you' might mean 'I'd like to give you some meat'.

The young female reaches down and picks up a bird's egg to offer to her prospective mate, exchanging a gift for the meat she has been given, and confirming her goodwill with eye contact. It is a sign of the trust that is to build up between them, and it is thought that *ergaster* are the first hominids to

The evolution of the whites of the eyes enabled one *ergaster* to understand more clearly the thoughts and intentions of another.

develop a strange new mutation that helps that process of reassurance. It is likely that they are the human ancestors who first had visible white sclera – the whites of the eyes – just like us. Perhaps this arose as individuals began to get an insight into the fact that other individuals had thoughts and feelings like they did. This simple feature of the eye has within it considerable power of communication, because it clearly exposes the direction of the gaze, and opens a window into the thoughts of the mind. The intent communicated in the direction of a glance can reveal whether you are looking into the eyes of a trusted friend or a deceitful enemy.

Despite the emergence of a co-operative society, direct physical conflict played an important role in the lives of *ergaster*. Hands, feet and teeth would all be used as weapons.

149

Suddenly the young male starts back, looking up into the tree above him, and his face distorts into a snarl. There above him, hidden until now by the branches and leaves, is another male – not just an apparent rival, but an interloper to the group. The confrontation is instant, and intense, betraying the fact of *ergaster*'s closeness to its ape origins. The gentle scene of courtship is transformed into a screaming, gesticulating frenzy of physical activity. No uninvited male is welcome, but for some males – like this interloper – the high-risk strategy of trying to enter another group can bring rich rewards. If they are lucky enough to bond with one of the unattached females, they will be accepted and gain access to the security offered by their new 'family'.

So at first he stands his ground, gesturing, trying to declare his innocence. But the noise and commotion soon bring over others of the group, and he is quickly surrounded by them. His behaviour changes, trying to convey penitence, looking away submissively from the circle of angry *ergaster;* but it is to no avail. Suddenly the attack on him comes, first, surprisingly, from the old female, and then immediately from the older male, whose great strength is expressed by a massive blow to the interloper's body. After brief moments of confused movement, the interloper manages to break free and runs off into the bush, while the others scream after him.

As the group settles to a semblance of calm, with occasional cries of anger echoing across the dunes, the young male hunter looks with gratitude towards the older member of the group, who has exercised his natural authority, but has nonetheless helped him out of trouble. The group has bonded that bit closer with the successful expulsion of an enemy; the older male basks in the admiration that comes his way, but the younger male has also had his position underlined as a valued member of the troop.

The group has bonded that bit closer with the successful expulsion of an enemy

(OPPOSITE) The threat of an interloper was dealt with harshly, as in many primate species.

151

It was a migration of over 10,000 kilometres (6,000 miles)

THE GREAT MIGRATION

Ergaster's command of the environment within which it has evolved, its ability to plan, to think ahead, to manage the complexity of its relationships, and the strength of the society that has developed to support it, have all made it the most successful hominid so far to have walked the Earth. And it has also been given the confidence to reach out further from its African origins. *Ergaster* has the ability to move into another, unfamiliar landscape, and to read the signs that will enable it to survive there, and this ability means that it has come to dominate the world, like no other species before it.

Although *ergaster* first appeared in Africa only about 1.9 million years before the present day, within less than 200,000 years its descendants had begun to migrate into the Middle East and on to the edge of Europe and to Asia. The creature that undertook that journeying is known as *Homo erectus,* and is almost identical to *ergaster,* but with thicker skull bones, and a more pronounced brow-ridge. *Erectus* moved across whole new continents and through whole new environments, north up the Nile valley, up through Sinai, and further north to the Black Sea. Others spread east, skirting the mountains of the Horn of Africa, across the coastal deserts of the Red Sea, over the land bridge that was the Gulf of Aden, along the dust plains of the Iranian coast, across India and around the foothills of the fledgling Himalayas, and into the steamy jungles of south-east Asia, to leave fossil remains in Java. Still others branched off north, eventually to arrive in China.

It was a migration of over 10,000 kilometres (6,000 miles) but, while the journey is indeed epic, in terms of human evolution – given *erectus*'s abilities – it is not in fact as remarkable as it sounds. As populations grew, so the offspring might need to move on, to

(PREVIOUS PAGE) *Homo ergaster* was smart enough to adapt to almost any environment. He and his immediate descendant *Homo erectus* undertook the first great hominid migration out of Africa.

(OPPOSITE) *Homo erectus* had only slight differences in appearance from ergaster. Together these species dominated the world for the best part of two million years.

The missing link goes missing

From the moment that Charles Darwin's theory of evolution by natural selection took the world by storm in the mid-1800s, the search for the 'missing link' between apes and men was on. The man with the first claim to having found it was a Dutchman called Eugene Dubois, who was just a year old when Darwin published in 1859. Dubois qualified in medicine but then fell out with his professor and joined the Royal Dutch East Indies Army as a medical officer, sailing off to Sumatra with his wife and young baby. There, he persuaded the East Indies authorities to fund his passion to search for fossils.

With the help of two civil engineers and fifty convicts as labourers, Dubois searched for two years until with great good fortune, in October 1891, along the banks of the Solo River in Java, they found some fossils partly exposed by the eroding shore. Their prize was a tooth and the skull cap of a hominid with low forehead and thick brow-ridge, and a brain size halfway between ape and human. The following spring they found a piece of thigh-bone. Dubois named it Pithecanthropus erectus, 'upright ape-man' – the missing link. This was the first discovery of Homo erectus, and it became popularly known as Java Man.

In Europe, his find was greeted with derision, and dismissed as a stray collection of the skull of a giant gibbon, the leg of a human, and a tooth that had nothing to do with either. Dubois became bitter and secretive, and eventually kept

The skull of Java Man.

the fossils hidden away from the scrutiny of his academic rivals. He died in 1940, and his gravestone is marked with a skull and crossbones.

It was a young Canadian doctor, Davidson Black, who found the next example of *erectus*. Although Dubois had not been accepted, most scientists now believed that Asia was the likely cradle of mankind, and so Black set off to China in search of early humans. His day job was teaching anatomy at Peking University, for which he was sent a supply of executed convicts to be used for dissection. When he complained that this was not right, he was sent live convicts instead! But to the initial intense disapproval of the Rockefeller Foundation, which paid his salary, Black's real interest was excavating the exotic cave of Zhoukoudian, near Peking (now Beijing). And there in 1929 he unearthed the skull cap of Peking Man. Thereafter, the scale of the excavation became huge, with up to 200 people gradually working

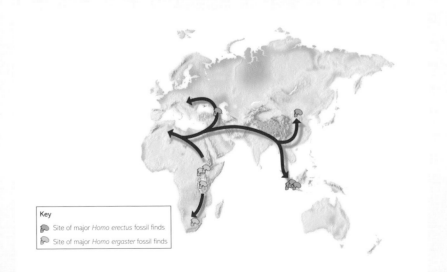

Key

Site of major *Homo erectus* fossil finds

Site of major *Homo ergaster* fossil finds

Homo ergaster and its descendant *homo erectus* undertook a 10,000 kilometre migration out of Africa.

Eugene Dubois (centre, standing) at Cambridge in 1898.

their way through the soils, so that Zhoukoudian yielded many more fragments of *erectus* over the next decade – although Black himself died young in 1934.

The excavations were brought to an end by the Japanese invasion of China at the start of the Second World War. The fossils of Peking Man were packed away for safekeeping, each lovingly wrapped in tissue and gauze, packed in wooden boxes, and padded inside large crates. It was agreed that the American ambassador would get them out of the country, and they were taken as part of the personal belongings of a Colonel William Ashurst, escorted by nine marines, on a train to the coast, to sail out on an American ship. They left Peking safely, and arrived at the coast on 7 December 1941 – the day of Pearl Harbor, the surprise Japanese attack on the American fleet. Twenty-four hours earlier and they would have been safe, but instead the train was intercepted and the fossils disappeared. Not even the Japanese occupiers could trace them.

All that remains of Peking Man are the casts that were made of the fossils, and one stone tool that was found with the remains. A tantalizing photograph of what seem like fossils in a box surfaced in the early 1970s, when a mysterious woman claimed to possess them, and demanded half a million dollars in ransom for their return. A first rendezvous was set at the top of the Empire State Building, but the woman fled after handing over the picture, and she was never traced.

The significance of Java Man and Peking Man is that together they reveal the extraordinary spread of colonization of the planet by *Homo erectus*. This species of hominid must have been truly adaptable to the very different environments that it encountered on its journey across the globe. Because meat was an important part of their diet they were no longer tied to the location of particular kinds of plants, so they could easily move. And move they did, generation by generation. In geological terms, this first great migration out of Africa was astonishingly quick. *Homo ergaster* fossils first appear in Africa just after two million years ago, but in 1994 two American scientists applied a new dating technique to some of the Java fossils and discovered they were 1.8 million years old, twice as old as originally thought. *Erectus* had already reached Asia by that time. It seems that from the moment it emerged, *ergaster* was intelligent enough to survive in new and different circumstances, and needed to move.

But further dating work has revealed something more remarkable. *Erectus* fossils found at Ngandong in Indonesia have now been dated to as recent as less than 50,000 years ago. If this work is correct, and more tests have seemed to support it, then *Homo erectus* was still going strong in Asia even after modern humans had emerged in Africa. To have inhabited the planet for two million years means *erectus* must take the prize for the most successful hominid that has ever lived.

ensure plenty of food for everyone. If each generation simply moved its basic camp a mere one kilometre (just over half a mile) further on, then the journey would easily be accomplished in the time. But the journey was made, and by the time the generations of offspring had worked their way across a quarter of the globe, they had adapted to new environments, and were thriving across the planet.

Little is different between *ergaster* and *erectus*, but for one puzzling thing. The refined stone tools that were such a feature of the African *ergaster* never made their appearance with *erectus* in Asia. It seems that the first hominids to migrate took with them the primitive stone tools of the time, and never came to develop anything more sophisticated: why?

(BELOW AND OPPOSITE) The bamboo forests of south-east Asia may have provided *erectus* with the means to make a variety of tools.

TOOLS OF THE FOREST

It is the middle of the day, but a shadow hangs over the face of the creature that is treading carefully through the dense undergrowth. Above him are the thick green leaves of a tropical forest canopy, with the sun only fleetingly forcing its way through to the ground.

Around him are the tall stems of a tough flexible wood, which makes progress through this jungle slow and painful. He is surrounded by bamboo. This is a world very different from that of the *ergaster* clan we have come to know, but this hominid is in his familiar element. At first glance he is indistinguishable from the *ergaster*, but his face is thicker set, and in one crucial respect he is different: he has a paler skin, probably reflecting his life in the monsoon climate of south-east Asia. For this is China 1.2 million years ago, and the creature scrambling through the jungle is *Homo erectus*, the descendant of the first *ergaster*, who left Africa over half a million years before.

While searching for one form of food, *erectus* would not miss an opportunity to try anything that offered itself up along the way. All but the legs of this spider becomes a tasty morsel.

Clutched in his hand, and those of the companions who are moving swiftly behind him, are not flaked stone axes, for workable flints are rare in this landscape. Instead they are carrying the vicious, sharp points of bamboo sticks. Bamboo is a plant that *erectus* has learned to work into a variety of different implements: stabbing points and sharp-edged cutting blades. It is hard and strong and its splintered edges are razor sharp; it well serves the purpose of these forest hunters. Even today it is still being used as a material for everything from needles to the building of whole villages on stilts. But unlike stone, it will be discarded once used and will quickly rot away, to leave no trace for future scientists to discover.

The *erectus* suddenly starts back and pauses. He draws his hand across his face, wiping away a massive spider's web that he has inadvertently walked into. But as soon as he has got over the surprise, he immediately looks around for the source. There on the tree is a large fat spider, and in one swift movement *erectus* grabs it and puts it in his mouth. A quick bite and it is gone, with only the hairy legs being spat out in distaste. Like *ergaster* before him, *erectus* is a culinary opportunist. One of his companions is stripping a piece of bamboo to create a needle point, which he then sticks into the gap in some tree bark and stabs. He pulls out the bamboo needle, and on the end is a big fat grub. It too is quickly despatched as a snack.

But then the voice of the third *erectus* calls, and he rushes forward to join the others, now running, crouching, leaping, across the forest floor, until suddenly they stop. Crouching down, one of them sniffs at some fresh dung on the ground. They all remain still, listening, eyes alert and scouring the forest for signs of prey. Ahead of them a muntjac deer stares back, frozen with fear and anticipation.

Bamboo needles, bamboo blades and bamboo spears: *erectus* is a master of working bamboo, and the short stabbing sticks in their hands are deadly weapons. Like their African cousins, *erectus* have become supremely adaptable and responsive to the environments in which they find

The scavenging skills of *Homo erectus* would have been of little use when pitted against the three-metre tall ape, *Gigantopithecus*.

themselves, and these three are as at home in this steamy forest as were their ancestors in the open savannah of Africa. Slowly their bamboo weapons are raised for the kill. Once targeted, no animal stands much chance of escape from the hominids.

And then it is all over. With a crash of splintered wood and broken branches, an enormous creature lunges forward between the *erectus* and their prey. It is a *Gigantopithecus*, a huge ape 3 metres (10 feet) tall. With a great bellow, it charges the group, who turn, fleeing in panic, allowing one of their number to fall and be brushed aside by the charging ape. But the injured hominid is not left alone, and later on his companions help him revive with water from a bamboo-leaf cup. They may not be strong enough to overcome every creature in the forest, but in the long term their intelligence is set to outlast many other animals. *Gigantopithecus* will be long extinct before the day of *erectus* is over. Indeed, *erectus* is destined to live on in the Far East long after his ancestor *ergaster* has died out. *Erectus* will become the longest-living species of hominids ever to walk the Earth, thriving for almost two million years, his last traces dying out less than 50,000 years before today.

The Englishman who never was

The scientific establishment of Edwardian Britain had a nagging irritation. For the previous fifty years, everyone else had been finding important fossil pre-humans except them. The Germans had Neanderthal Man, the French had Cro-Magnon Man, the Dutch had Java Man, and now there was even a second German with Heidelberg Man (a huge jawbone found at the small German village of Mauer in 1907). In the heightened climate of pre-Great War Europe, Britain needed an early Englishman. In 1912 he was found, and he turned out to be not just any early Englishman, but a truly sensational fossil discovery.

Teilhard de Chardin, Charles Dawson and Sir Arthur Smith Woodward digging at Piltdown, with one of the estate workers in the background.

The story began that spring when Charles Dawson, a Sussex solicitor and amateur geologist, brought some pieces of old skull to the Natural History Museum in London. He explained that they had been found alongside some prehistoric elephant and hippopotamus teeth in a small gravel bed at Barkham Manor, near Piltdown Common in Sussex, where Dawson was the manor steward. The museum's keeper of geology, Arthur Smith Woodward, immediately saw the significance of the find. Throughout the summer, he and Dawson, along with the renowned palaeontologist and cleric, Father Teilhard de Chardin, dug further at the site, finding something new on almost every day they worked. They uncovered more parts of the skull, teeth from a prehistoric horse and mastodon, and a plethora of other ancient creatures that proved the antiquity of the find.

Finally, they uncovered a lower jaw, which completely astonished them. While the skull had been shaped like that of a human, the jaw was like that of an ape. This was quite the opposite of all previous early human finds (like Neanderthal and Java Man): he had a large brain, but also a huge ape-like jaw. It must have meant that the large human brain had evolved long before we had shaken off our ape-like original features. More importantly, it meant that this English fossil must have marked the true line of our ancestry: not Cro-Magnon, not Java Man, not the Neanderthals. The

announcement of the find in December 1912 was a scientific sensation.

Over the following summers more material was found, including, miraculously, the canine tooth that had been missing from the jaw, and a fragment of elephant thigh bone that had been worked. It was shaped rather like a cricket bat and was clearly a bone implement fashioned by the ape-man, and confirmation of his superior intelligence.

Dawson died in 1916, but *Eoanthropus dawsoni* – Dawson's Dawn Man – lived on in the world of heated academic dispute. Over the years Piltdown Man, as the find became known, provoked much debate, and gradually began to look more and more out of keeping with other early hominids that were found, with their low foreheads and large brow-ridges. Eventually it became viewed as the great British find that no one spoke about very much, until during the 1940s serious questions began to be asked about its authenticity. Smith Woodward died in 1948, believing in Piltdown to the end, dictating his book *The Earliest Englishman* on his deathbed. But just five years later, new chemical techniques of dating fossils had come into use, and in 1953 a series of tests revealed that the remains were no more than 500 years old, and had been stained with iron and chromium to make them look ancient.

The human-like skull was simply a human skull. The ape-like jaw was also

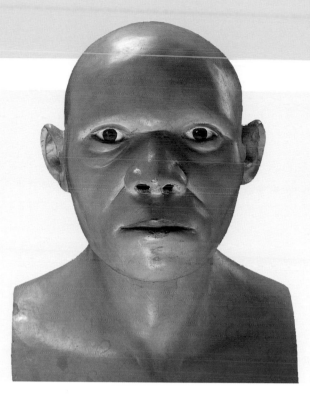

(LEFT) A bust of the Piltdown Man as he was imagined to have looked, with large forehead and prominent jaw.

(RIGHT) The Piltdown jaw was in fact that of an orang-utan, with the teeth filed flat, to emulate human wear.

exactly what it seemed: the jaw of an orang-utan, with the teeth filed flat to emulate human wear. The canine tooth (another ape's) had been filed to shape and painted with artist's Van Dyke brown. As for the 'cricket bat', whoever had shaped it had used a steel knife, and evidently had a very English sense of humour.

The exposure of the fraud was almost a relief for the scientific community, who by then had confined Piltdown Man to a drawer in the museum where its awkwardness could not be dwelled upon. But ever since then speculation has raged as to who was the perpetrator of the fraud. Was it Dawson himself, always the prime suspect, or was it Teilhard de Chardin, who had befriended Dawson shortly after the original pieces were found? Was it Samuel Woodhead, the principal of the local Agricultural College, who had advised Dawson on how to 'harden' fossil bones with chemicals?

Was it Lewis Abbott, a jeweller in Hastings, who had looked after the skull fragments for Dawson, and who possessed all the intricate skills to work on the filing of teeth and bones? Was it even Sir Arthur Conan Doyle, the great creator of Sherlock Holmes, who lived locally, was an acquaintance of Dawson, and who was known to have visited the site? Or was it someone within the Natural History Museum who held an academic grudge against Smith Woodward, and wished to show him up as a fool?

Many tantalizing clues, remarks recalled from childhood, ambiguous letters and cryptic notes have been handed down over the years, each one purporting to prove the identity of the hoaxer. However, in 1996 it was announced that the 'smoking gun' in the case might at last have been found. A canvas travelling trunk had been discovered in the roof space at the

Natural History Museum in the mid-1970s, and it contained a number of assorted bones, stained in an identical way to the Piltdown remains. The initials on the trunk were M.A.C.H, and inside was correspondence belonging to Martin Hinton, who was a curator of zoology at the museum around the time of the fraud. It seems perhaps that Hinton had used these other bones to practise the staining technique before planting the Piltdown pieces. It also turns out that he was well known as a practical joker, and also bore a grudge against Smith Woodward, because of a dispute over funding his work, so a motive for the fraud might well lie there.

However, just because Hinton worked on the staining technique does not actually prove he was the forger, and so the longest running, most infamous and embarrassing case of fraud in British science is unlikely to be brought to an end just yet.

SETTLING DOWN

Back in Africa, we find our *ergaster* group once again, settled at their camp as the sun is setting. But now they have moved on from the baking mudflat, and have also moved on in time. The cry of a baby is heard, and the older male hunter strokes the head of the newborn infant that he rests on his lap, while his partner is quietly grooming his hair. Further away the old female is playing with another grandchild; with the help of the grandmother, the female will soon be

The young male and female have now formed a pair, and they are likely to stay together at least until some time after their first child has been weaned.

able to produce more young, although by now she is bonding with a different male. The young male and female are now clearly a pair, sitting away from the others expressing occasional simple words to each other. Surprisingly, on the very edge of the group, the interloper is now squatting, chanting to himself while knapping at a hand-axe. He is on the periphery of the group and is not yet fully part of their lives, but through persistence and a slow build-up of trust he has become accepted as a presence. He now has security, and the group will have a new strong male to help support their numbers.

A single spark of imagination was enough to transform their lives.

The adaptability and intelligence shown by *ergaster* and *erectus* in moving out of Africa will allow them to dominate the rest of the world for a million years or more. But we should not assume too many powers of imagination on their part. For, although they have invented and perfected the most advanced stone cutting tool yet seen, the Acheulean hand-axe, they and their descendants will make no new change to its design, and no improvement to its function for all of those million years. For them, the axe must have emerged from an evolutionary need to have better tools. But now it works well for everything they need, so there is no pressure to do anything different. Their world is settled, so they have no need to change a thing. In a million years, their technology – and so their brains – will not advance by one degree. It will not even occur to them to do something as basic as fit an axe-head on to the end of a stick to make a spear.

In modern times we have gone from the Wright Brothers' first powered flight to space exploration in less than a hundred years. *Ergaster* and their descendants have come up with nothing new in a million. It is hard to understand such a lack of ingenuity. They simply cannot imagine that life could be different, and perhaps it is that lack of creative imagination that in the end marks them out as being not fully human.

Whenever the moment was that its use came into the human repertoire, fire became a basic part of life.

However, it is likely that there was one further major advance during the time of *ergaster* and *erectus*. We will never know precisely where it happened or when, but remains of clay and soil baked at campfire temperatures, found near animal fossils and in caves, have provided tantalizing clues that as early as 1.4 million years ago, or perhaps as late as half a million, our ancestors encountered fire in a very different way. Unlike all other creatures, and all of their ancestors before them, they did not back away. There was a moment when one of them saw that they could use it. And that single spark of intelligence was enough to transform their lives, and to bequeath enormous power to all of their descendants.

They would often have seen fire before, and come close to it, following natural lightning strikes, or bush fires started by the smouldering of parched grass in the heat of summer on the savannah. But this was different. It was possibly many thousands of generations on before the hominids learned to actually create fire, and it is uncertain which of them or their descendants it was who achieved that remarkable feat. But once fire was there before them, they learned to harness it, and to control it. Warmth for survival, a weapon for protection against animals, or perhaps even the cooking of food: the advantages of fire were legion. Whenever the moment was that its use came into the human repertoire, fire became a basic part of life. Perhaps as they gathered round the blaze, our distant ancestors experienced something of the primeval feeling that we all still seem to share today, as we let our minds wander, staring into the flames of an open fire. We will never know, but perhaps this may have set in train the next stage in our evolution, the birth of the characteristics that really mark out modern humans from all other species: our creativity and our imagination.

(OPPOSITE) The harnessing of fire was the single most significant act that demonstrated early humans had begun to take control of the world they lived in.

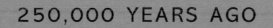

250,000 YEARS AGO

The Survivors

4

Southern England, 400,000 years ago: a large man is seated on a low tree-lined hill overlooking a grassy plain, which is peppered by large boulders. He is staring ahead, thinking. His ancestral relatives have inhabited these northern European lands for some 350,000 years before him. He is the product of thousands of generations of adaptation to the world in which he lives, and his lineage has survived the most bleak, hostile and unpredictable environment that hominids have yet had to face. A million years after the long migration of *Homo ergaster* began out of Africa, archaic humans first reached Europe. Generation by generation *ergaster*'s descendants had travelled, each family seeking that little bit of extra territory, moving further than the last, hill by hill, valley by valley and river bed by river bed. By 1.8 million years ago their descendants had journeyed slowly and steadily through the Middle East, and to the north around the vast Black Sea. They had travelled eastwards to the Far East, where they lived on, almost unchanging, until very recent times, as *Homo erectus*.

But *ergaster*'s descendants also spread into western Europe, by a route of which we are never likely to be certain, and they arrived there about 800,000 years before the present day. Those first Europeans had already evolved into something new. Still long-limbed and tall, they had become stronger, hardier and smarter: still with the heavy brow-ridge and sloping forehead, but now with a larger cranium, and a bigger brain that offered far more ability to adapt to their new worlds. And they needed every scrap of cleverness they could muster, because by the time they were established in Europe, they faced a new pressure: harder weather.

For reasons that are still not clear, 2.6 million years ago the climate of the planet began to enter a period of general cooling, coupled with great instability, alternately cooling and warming with increasing frequency, so that huge swings of climate occurred. In Europe, the cold brought ice, with glaciers reaching out for many

they needed every scrap of cleverness they could muster

(OPPOSITE) A heavy brow-ridge and a broad face were the characteristics of the first Europeans, *Homo heidelbergensis*.

thousands of years, and then retreating as the climate warmed again, leaving the land scoured and littered with boulders. From 800,000 years ago Europe was predominantly a cold world, but there were also eras of warmth known as interglacials. This was the world that the European hominids came to know, and learned to survive in.

But none of these thoughts are entering the head of our grim-faced hunter. Indeed, he is not capable of thoughts of that depth. His mind is focused on only one thing: his plan for the kill that is about to play out in the trees at the edge of the plain below. Clutching a wooden spear and rising silently to his feet, he signals to two companions, and the three men begin to move slowly forward, part crouching, through the tall grass. A short distance ahead, the object of their attention is grazing. It is a giant Irish elk, or *Megaloceros*, and as it feeds in the early morning sun it glances round, pausing, nervously sniffing for danger. On their leader's signal, the hunters fan out, being careful to remain upwind of the creature. Patiently, they stalk it, until finally they are in range. Hiding behind a huge

Tall, agile, very strong, and with the intelligence to make finely-balanced wooden spears, *Homo heidelbergensis* were formidable hunters.

stone, the leader stands, arches back his muscular arm and launches his throwing spear. The others follow suit, hurling a volley of weapons with deadly force.

These brothers are *Homo heidelbergensis*, and they are perhaps the most recognizably 'human' species yet to have set foot on Earth. They are armed with all the attributes that have proved so successful in hominids up to now: the ability to walk upright, the ability to take a flexible approach to life, and the capacity to thrive within large, intricate societies. They have begun to dominate their world to an extent never seen before. This attack on the Irish elk is no opportunistic stalking and scavenging of a dying animal, but a thought-through strategy for killing. These men are strong, confident in their ability, and unafraid of taking on the largest and most fearsome of other animals as prey.

At this time, 400,000 years ago, the climate of Europe is in one of the interglacial periods that have become characteristic of the planet. The ice sheets have retreated far to the north, and southern England

(OVERLEAF) The antlers of the *Megaloceros* were formidable weapons of defence, and the hunters need to rely on their wits as well as their skill with the spear.

The Pit of Bones

One of the great challenges of explaining the origin of humans is that there is really very little hard evidence remaining of a story that has lasted over six million years. This means that almost every new find makes a dramatic contribution to the building up of theories. Once in a while there are truly spectacular discoveries that completely alter what we know about our past.

The Pit of Bones is one such site. Accessible only after a long struggle through underground caves and tunnels in the limestone hills of Atapuerca in northern Spain, the chamber lies at the bottom of a 15 (50-foot) shaft deep within the hill. It was discovered by potholers in 1976. The cave system had been used extensively as a den by cave bears, and buried under a heap of their bones were found fragments of hominid teeth and skull. For the next six years, archaeologists struggled to remove the tons of sediment and bear bones, carrying the rubbish to the surface in their rucksacks, until they could properly excavate the chamber. They could work for only a few hours each day before the air ran out in the cramped underground space, with five people at a time sitting on wooden planks suspended over the floor. But the excavations since then have turned up the remains of thirty-two individual early humans dating from around 300,000 years ago. Indeed, so rich has been the find that it now accounts for 75 per cent of all the known hominid fossils between 100,000 and 1.5 million years ago.

The fossils date from the time when Europe was populated by *Homo heidelbergensis*, and they have provided a wealth of detail of what the creatures were like. Archaeologists have found a whole skull, ribs, backbone, arms, knees, feet, hands, fingers and toes. The people were tall and sturdy, with very large noses, no chin, but prominent brow-ridges and a wide face. They showed some of the same physical features characteristic of *Homo ergaster* from Africa, but at the same time revealed clear similarities with the Neanderthals who were to follow them within the next 50,000 years. It seems likely therefore that *heidelbergensis* was a descendant of *ergaster*, and in turn gave rise to the Neanderthals.

Why are the skeletons in the pit, and how did they get there? There are no remains of any other animals from their time, so it seems unlikely that they were victims dragged there by lions or other carnivores. Instead, it seems more likely that the bodies were deliberately thrown in there by their fellows. They are also almost all the bodies of adolescents, with only two adults and a child having been found. The lead scientist of the Spanish research team, Professor Juan Luis Arsuaga, also believes that the bodies come from one group, and came to rest there over a period of maybe only a year. Many of them also show signs of disease: bone disease, possible infection from broken teeth, growths in the ear and symptoms of malnourishment. One

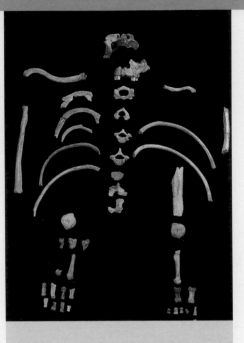

The skeleton of the species named *Homo antecessor* by Spanish scientists, found at Trinchera Dolina.

possibility is that they were all struck down by illness of varying kinds and their bodies were dumped in the pit.

But more than that, the pit has also thrown up some strange and unexpected evidence that may illuminate a darker side of these early humans. Close examination of some of the bones reveals cut-marks: the signs of defleshing by stone tools. Professor Arsuaga suggests that this is strong evidence for cannibalism among the *heidelbergensis*.

Cannibalism could be either part of a ritual process, or simply a way of getting nourishment, but there is no further evidence either way. No other *heidelbergensis* sites have ever turned up evidence for any ritual or creative behaviour, beyond the making of stone tools, so perhaps the more mundane explanation is the most likely. The corpses were defleshed because the living needed food. If so, it does not mean that these early humans could not feel sad for the death of their friends or family. It is just that they would focus on the practical steps that would follow from death, rather than any spiritual concern.

Barely a few hundred metres from the Atapuerca cavern that houses the Pit of Bones, the scientists unearthed another remarkable find. From an old railway cutting at a site called Gran Dolina, in 1994 they discovered some crude stone tools and bones dating from 780,000 years ago, which makes them the earliest known hominid fossils in western Europe. In particular, the discovery has refined the ancestral role

of *Homo ergaster* in human evolution. A premolar tooth and the brow-ridge of a child's skull were both very similar to that of *ergaster*.

The Spanish scientists have named these early Europeans *Homo antecessor*, and believe that their physical traits show that they were a separate species, descended from *ergaster*, but which in due course gave rise to the *heidelbergensis* that later dominated the continent. These discoveries at Atapuerca seem to underline the evolutionary importance of *ergaster*, and its position at the start of perhaps several waves of migration of its descendants out of Africa.

Above all, Atapuerca has shown that Europe was populated by hominids from

a time much earlier than had previously been thought possible. But it seems to be a consistent fact of life for all palaeoanthropological discoveries that they tend to push the key moments in hominid evolution further and further back in time. In the summer of 2002, an announcement came of the re-dating of some animal bones found at a hominid site in East Anglia in England. The new result had come out at over 700,000 years ago. This was over 200,000 years earlier than the first Britons were thought to have lived. It seems that our ancestors had thrived not only in the warmth of Spain but right across a much wider range of Europe, for far longer than we had believed.

These *Homo heidelbergensis* remains from Atapuerca, photographed in situ, include two skulls.

Homo heidelbergensis

Male *Homo heidelbergensis.*

Who discovered *heidelbergensis*?

The first, and for a long time only, *Homo heidelbergensis* fossil was an enigmatic jawbone found in sandpits near the village of Mauer, south-east of Heidelberg in Germany. It was the culmination of a twenty-year search by a palaeontologist called Otto Shoetensack, who was sure that remains of prehistoric men would be found there. A workman discovered the 'Heidelberg jaw' in 1907, although at first it was thought to be a primitive Neanderthal. It was not until 1921 that a skull of the species was found, this time in a cave in Broken Hill at Kabwe, in what is now Zambia. Since then, several skulls have been found, as well as other fragments of skeleton, such as the Boxgrove shin-bone (see the feature on pages 182–3).

When did *heidelbergensis* live?

The earliest certain *heidelbergensis* is the Bodo Cranium from Ethiopia, dating from around 600,000 years ago. As such, it stands at a crossroads of human evolution. It is the strongest candidate for being the ancestor to both Neanderthals and modern humans. No *heidelbergensis* finds later than 250,000 years ago have been uncovered, by which time the Neanderthals were already spreading throughout the same territory that it had come to inhabit.

Where did *heidelbergensis* live?

Heidelberg Man has been found throughout East Africa and Europe. It was the first creature to colonize the colder climate of northern Europe, and recent discoveries in Britain suggest that it had spread even further and earlier than had been thought previously (see the feature on pages 182–3). Features of skeletons found in Spain, from almost 800,000 years ago, show striking similarities with *heidelbergensis* and also *ergaster*, suggesting a clear line of descent, and their discoverers want to define these very early Europeans as a new species, *Homo antecessor* (see the feature on pages 176–7). However, this is the subject of considerable debate among scientists.

What did *heidelbergensis* look like?

The Bodo Cranium has the largest human face in the known hominid fossil record. Another fossil *heidelbergensis* has the widest nose. The males were very big creatures, standing 180 centimetres (nearly 6 feet) tall and weighing 80 kilograms (12$^{1}/_{2}$ stone), with very thick bones that required a strong set of muscles and sinews to support them. The females were slightly smaller, but both sexes were very strong. The body was essentially human, but the skull still had prominent brow ridges and a long sloping forehead. However, the brain was much larger than ergaster's at around 1,250 cubic centimetres (76 cubic inches). This is close to that of a modern human, although it was lacking in the area of the neocortex. *Heidelbergensis* teeth were fifty per cent longer than modern human ones, and crowded the jawbone, so that the bone sloped back from the front of the face, leaving no chin.

How would *heidelbergensis* have lived?

Heidelbergensis teeth were coated with a thick layer of enamel, which suggests that they were adapted to an abrasive diet, and could deal with chewing the tough sinews of large animals. Patterns of wear also suggest that they used their teeth as a 'third hand' to hold implements while they worked with them. Their use of stone tools and wooden spears (see the feature on pages 182-3) reveals that they were accomplished hunters. Their strength and brainpower would have equipped them to deal with the large and violent game faced. There is some evidence that they were the first hominids to live in crudely made shelters.

is a temperate land dominated by large animals – megafauna – that graze on a rich flora, and which are themselves the prey of other strong carnivores. As well as the giant deer, there are horse, rhinoceros, elephant and hippopotamus; there are wolves, lions and other big cats; there are hares, shrews, voles, bats and hedgehogs; in the sky there are geese, ducks, gulls, great auks and robins; in the rivers and along the seashores there are salmon, newts, toads, eels and even blue fin tuna. For now, it is a good land in which to live. But it is also full of danger.

Baying with the pain of the spears sticking into its side, the *Megaloceros* breaks into a run. But the *heidelbergensis* remain calm, waiting for the wounded animal to slow. Sure enough, gravely injured, it stiffens, and gradually collapses to the ground. Seeing this, the men rush forward, their faces a picture of aggression. Their bodies are extraordinarily powerful. Over 180 centimetres (around 6 feet) tall, thick-boned and muscular, they are massively built and fearsomely strong. As they charge, they call out to each other strange words that mean 'Attack, attack!' They have developed a very basic language, with simple nouns and verbs. Its only use is to help them with concepts that are rooted firmly in the present, rather than think about any deeper history. But communicating ideas in the present is an advantage nonetheless. These hominids can think of tactics, and use them as a team.

> They have developed a very basic language, with simple nouns and verbs.

Two of the brothers distract the *Megaloceros* at the front, while the third, the youngest, creeps closer from behind clutching a heavier stabbing spear, and tries to strike the thrashing animal in the neck. But it is a very dangerous move. With one last effort, the giant deer staggers back to its feet, a huge terrified animal twice the height of the men, with antlers that splay out over three metres (ten feet) wide. Its weakness means that its only defence is to wave its antlers from side to side, but that alone is enough to do damage, and the jagged blades audibly swoosh as they curve through the air. The young

Homo heidelbergensis cared for their sick and injured, and would have been fearful for their safety, but they would have had no interest in them once they had died.

heidelbergensis has to jump back more than once to avoid getting hit, and suddenly he loses his footing. He is athletic and agile, and is off balance only for a few moments, but it is enough. With a sickening crack, the vast antlers deal him a savage blow across his head.

Roused to a rage by this turn of events, the remaining two *heidelbergensis* move in suddenly to finish the animal off. The leader stabs it repeatedly – angry beyond control – until the creature lies dead. Then, chests heaving with the exertions of the chase, the two men pause. One bends to his fallen comrade, to inspect the damage done by the deer, while the other sets about the skilful task of butchering the dead animal with his sharp stone hand-axe.

By nightfall the hunters have returned to their camp at the edge of the woodland. Here, hunks of meat lie wrapped in skin on the ground, and the group of *heidelbergensis* is gathered around a burning campfire. They are eating hungrily, and would be relaxed but for one thing. their injured brother is semi-conscious, oozing blood from a deep gash in his head. He too is wrapped in an animal skin, half sitting, half lying, resting in the arms of a female who is making gentle rhythmic sounds over him, a noise that might one day be called singing. The leader is squatting nearby, chewing herbs, which he packs into the wound. They are clearly anxious and restless, because this injured man is a strong young hunter, and the group knows it will be weaker without him. But as the firelight gently dies into the night, so the young man's life slips away, and the two *heidelbergensis* who are tending him display an almost human show of grief for the loss.

In many ways, *heidelbergensis* seem very like us, with their familiar, if large, physique, their skills with tools, their ability to talk, however simply, and even their 'human' emotions. But there is something deeper that is very different, which is revealed by a behaviour that to us would seem unacceptable, and the following morning it becomes clear. Now, around the campfire there are only the signs of departure. The embers are almost cold, and scraps of wood and flaked stone lie everywhere. Piled to one side are the hacked remnants of the meat and bones the hominids were sharing, but sitting at the edge of the empty circle that marks the human occupation there remains only one man. Hunched up and still, his head resting on his knees, he is dead. The injured hunter has been left precisely where he died, and the others have moved on, carrying their meat, stones and spears with them across the wooded plain.

For modern humans, it would be unthinkable to leave our dead in this way, and to show no reverence for the body of someone who was once a valued relative or friend. But for *heidelbergensis*, it would be unthinkable not to leave him. For the *heidelbergensis* mind still lacks the ability to look beyond the world of the every day, or beyond the knowledge and memories needed to survive and thrive in the tough world around them. Concepts of who they are, and what might happen to them in the far future, simply do not enter their heads.

The injured hunter has been left precisely where he died

The hunters of Boxgrove

West Sussex in England has turned out to provide a rich source of evidence as to how the earliest Europeans spent their time, and the skills they developed to stay alive. Boxgrove today is a gravel quarry, one side of which features a tall cliff, revealing sediments of chalk, flint and brick earth. Half a million years ago, however, it was a chalk cliff and a beach, with a tidal lagoon sheltering behind a headland, and home to a very busy group of people. For over a decade in the 1980s and 1990s, a team of mostly volunteers led by archaeologist Mark Roberts uncovered a wealth of prehistoric remains of its occupation. At that time, the area was basking in the warm climate of an interglacial period, and there was a wide range of animals inhabiting it: cave bear, wolf, rhinoceros, horse, giant deer, mountain hares, voles, frogs, fish and birds. It was a great place to find meat.

As well as the remains of animals, the Boxgrove site has turned up tens of thousands of examples of flint and bone tools. The demands of the hunt were so great that cutting blades, slashing blades, axes, slicing knives and a host of other stone implements were made in vast numbers. At one part of the site the 'flint shadow' of a man was found: the outline of his legs as he sat on the ground making tools, perhaps all day, flaking stone relentlessly, so that a shower of tiny fragments fell on and around him, marking out the position of his limbs on the ground. Effectively it was a flint

factory. A hammer carved from a deer antler was found to be embedded with many fragments of flint, confirming the technique of finishing the fine stone hand-axes by hitting them with a soft bone tool.

Then in 1993 a shin-bone of the man himself was found: Boxgrove Man. Measuring 35 centimetres (just over 1 foot) long, it was from an extraordinarily tall and well built male, and it was soon realized that the people who had inhabited the coastal settlement were a type of *Homo heidelbergensis*, descendants of the first inhabitants of Europe.

Two years later two hominid teeth were discovered, though no other human remains. But it was from the tools and animal bones that the picture of *heidelbergensis* life was built up. In several places the remains of complete animal carcasses were found, and these were no trivial amounts of meat. There was a complete horse, and two rhino, each of which would have weighed some 700 kilograms (getting on for three-quarters of a ton). Yet clearly they had been carried back to the camp from wherever they had died. Closer examination of the bones revealed a pattern of flint cut-marks, showing that they had been butchered with great care and skill. On the rhinos, almost every available piece of meat had been carved away: the lines left by the stone blades showed how even the neck fillets had been removed. But perhaps the most

This tibia (shin-bone) created a sensation when it was discovered in 1993. At almost 500,000 years old, and massive in its proportions and strength, it is a formidable specimen of the earliest known hominid in Britain – Boxgrove Man.

significant mark was where the teeth of other carnivores, particularly wolves, had also chewed at the animal bones. The tooth marks appeared on top of the marks from the butcher's blade. The implication is that the hominids got there first: the humans actually made the kill.

Boxgrove is not the only site in Europe where the world of *Homo heidelbergensis* has been brought to life. At Bilzingsleben in Germany, a site has been found which could be evidence of an even more sophisticated lifestyle. Dated at between 320,000 and 410,000 years old, there are what look like stones used as anvils on which to break up large animal bones, and bits of bone shaped to make long blades for scraping animal hides. These interpretations are still in debate, and most controversial of all is the interpretation of circular patterns of bones and stones as the rubbish left around the edge of crude huts. If this is correct, then it is a sign of the beginnings of an organized community, with the hunters supplying meat for other people who worked back at the base camp.

But there is definite evidence of the hunters' skill elsewhere. Also in Germany, near Heidelberg itself, the place that gave *heidelbergensis* its original name, there is an open-strip coal mine at Schöningen. This mine has turned up nine almost miraculously preserved samples of *heidelbergensis* handiwork. Looking as if they were crafted only yesterday, but dated by the layers of the mine to around 400,000 years ago, they are shiny polished wooden spears. Each was cut from the trunk of a small spruce tree, with the point sharpened at the base, where the wood is strongest. Each is over two metres (six feet) long, and finely balanced to be thrown through the air like a javelin. And back at Boxgrove, the shoulder blade of a deer was found with a round hole broken through it. An experiment with a pointed wooden spear revealed that a spear-throw was the likely cause of the injury to the animal.

All of this evidence together has built up a clear picture of hominid life half a million years ago. Whereas their ancestors had scavenged meat from the kills of other animals, or at best despatched a sick or injured animal to a quicker end, these early Europeans were deliberate and effective hunters. They were confident of tackling large animals, unafraid of possible competition from other carnivores that roamed their land, and they were bringing down large quantities of big game to supply a major settlement. All of this would have required co-ordination. Everything in their behaviour therefore points to an ability to communicate precise plans. This argument, combined with their larger brain, leads scientists to be confident that some form of early language must have been in regular use by this time.

There is a final irony that Boxgrove lies so close to the site of the most famous scientific fraud of all time (see the feature on pages 162–3). This time, the gravel beds of Sussex have revealed a true picture of the earliest Europeans.

Excavation at the Boxgrove site.

Although they cared for the companion who hunted with them, now he is gone, and there is simply no benefit to them to linger with him. Their world is the here and now, the recent past and the immediate future. Imagination is something that has yet to evolve.

CLIMATE OF REASON

As is so often the case in the story of our origins, climate was a critical factor in setting the framework for our human imagination to emerge. By now, early humans were present on every continent except the Americas and the isolated world of Australia. The period of interglacial warmth had allowed *heidelbergensis* to establish itself throughout the northern lands. But the climate had begun to change, plummeting to a new and brutal era of ice cover.

In the north, the gradual arrival of the ice brought back the brutal, harsh world of cold. The warm-weather fauna disappeared: elephants gave way to the mammoth, and the hippos gave way to woolly rhino. The temperature fell by an average of 5°C (about 9°F). But this was just the beginning of a roller-coaster ride of the climate. Over the next 200,000 years the ice advanced and then retreated in the familiar cycles of cold and warm. Sometimes each of these eras could last for many thousands of years, but new scientific techniques have revealed that the climate was capable of changing from one state to the other very rapidly indeed, over as little as a few human lifetimes.

For the *heidelbergensis* at the start of this era the change was extreme: in just a few generations, the land where they had hunted game across open grassy plains and along wide river deltas became a sea of ice and snow. As the ice advanced and retreated, so populations of *heidelbergensis* abandoned and then recolonized the land. But ultimately, the pressure on these early humans meant that they had to adapt, and over 150,000 years or more, their descendants evolved into a new kind of human being: *Homo neanderthalensis* – the Neanderthals.

Before we meet these new and famous ancestral cousins, we will look at what the climate change had brought to another key part of the world: Africa. As the ice swept out across the northern

A *heidelbergensis* female.

Homo neanderthalensis

Who discovered *neanderthalensis*?

Unlike most of our ancestral relatives, *Homo neanderthalensis* has become more popularly known by its colloquial name: Neanderthal. The first fossil was discovered inside the Feldhofer Cave in the Neander Valley near Dusseldorf in Germany in 1856. The workmen who found it thought the bones were the remains of a bear, but the local schoolteacher recognized them as something unusual, and handed them over to an academic at the nearby university. He announced that they were the remains of one of the barbarian hordes that had overwhelmed Rome. Another suggestion was that it was only the body of a Cossack soldier who had died in pursuit of Napoleon's army in 1814. But eventually the Neanderthal skeleton was recognized as being a half-ape, half-human, distinctly separate species of *Homo*. It was the first 'other' kind of human being ever to be found.

When did *neanderthalensis* live?

The Neanderthals lived from at least 230,000 years until about 28,000 years ago (the estimated age of the most recent fossil found). It is likely that their ancestors were the European branch of *Homo heidelbergensis*, with a gradual transition between the two species occurring before about 300,000 years ago. During this long period, the world was undergoing many extreme changes in its climate.

Where did *neanderthalensis* live?

They were an extremely successful hominid species. Neanderthals were widespread across most of Eurasia. Their remains have been found in Russia, the Caucasus, Israel, the Balkans, central Europe, Germany, France, Italy and Spain, and as far north as Britain, but never in Africa or the Far East. As the climate of the northern hemisphere changed dramatically throughout their time on Earth, the populations of Neanderthal probably rose and fell. They would have abandoned some lands during extremes of climate, and then recolonized them when things got better. However, they were adaptable enough to live in a range of climates and environments.

What did *neanderthalensis* look like?

Their bodies had evolved to be adapted to the colder climate in which they lived. Although probably descended from the line of the tall *heidelbergensis*, the Neanderthals were squat and thickset, with a short, stockier body shape that would conserve heat most efficiently. Males were about 165 centimetres (5 feet 5 inches) tall, and females about 155 centimetres (5 feet 2 inches). They had very large noses, which would have been important for cooling the body during heavy exercise, to avoid sweat, which might freeze. A prominent brow-ridge and a receding forehead masked a very large brain — on average larger than our own. They had a receding chin.

Male *Homo neanderthalis*.

How would *neanderthalensis* have lived?

Neanderthals were highly skilled makers of refined stone tools, and it is clear that they were formidable hunters. The spears they created, the first to be tipped with stone blades, seem to have been designed exclusively for stabbing rather than throwing, so they tackled their prey at close quarters. Their lives were tough, and they lived to no more than thirty or forty years old on average. They cooked on hearths, and they made clothes. They lived in small groups of maybe as few as eight to ten, enabling them to cope with smaller food resources when times were hard. However, this approach meant the population as a whole could become more fragmented, and gene flow across it reduced. So the species was more vulnerable to extinction.

hemisphere, so more and more water was drawn out of the atmosphere and oceans to become locked up in the vast ice sheets and glaciers. Water that might once have rained from the skies remained firmly on the land as a solid. So, ironically, while the world was getting much colder, in the equatorial regions of Africa, where the ice never reached, it was getting very much drier. Africa became as parched as it could ever become, and the climate pressure on the early humans who lived there – very close cousins to the *heidelbergensis*, who had also evolved from *ergaster* – was very different, but equally as great. And from this drought-ridden land yet another kind of human emerged: *Homo sapiens* – us.

Of these two great species, only one would ultimately survive, and we of course know which one. But 150,000 years ago it was by no means certain what the outcome would be, for the Neanderthals were very successful indeed.

AN ICE AGE

Ice age Europe, 150,000 years ago, is a bleak land. The ice cap permanently covers most of the region, reaching south as far as southern England, creating a blanket two kilometres (over a mile) thick. The glaciers of the Alps spread out like tongues of cold across the central lands of France and Germany. And in between the sheets of ice lie vast swathes of frozen tundra that stretch from Denmark all the way to the French Riviera. It is a forbidding and unrelenting landscape, where only the hardiest forms of life survive, and the work required to stay alive is formidable.

Three Neanderthal men are picking their way along a vast lagoon of blue ice. They are wrapped in furs and are carrying spears. Fifteen thousand more generations under the evolutionary pressure of extreme climate change have transformed the descendants of *heidelbergensis*. No longer tall and long-limbed, the Neanderthals have evolved a shorter, stockier, altogether more solid physique that is well suited to their freezing world. The shorter, rounded shape provides less surface area for the body to lose valuable heat, when the temperatures around them can regularly reach as low as 30°C below freezing (-22°F).

Here, in what will become known as the Massif Central in France, the summer is drifting into autumn and the region is already blanketed with snow. These men left their group's camp the day before in search of food, and nothing has materialized until now. The leader of the three stops, turning his head this way and that, listening, and anxious, occasionally giving a rasping cough. With winter conditions setting in so early this year, many of the animals that they would normally hunt have already moved south, and meat is now scarce. He is in a dilemma: he knows that they should move south with the game, but he also wants to stay in the hope of

(ABOVE) Short and stocky, the Neanderthal body shape was supremely adapted to the ice age world.

(OVERLEAF) A hunt for food could involve trekking for days across the icy wasteland.

187

finding food, because for him the search has particular importance. Back at camp is a young woman, heavily pregnant with his child, and he is worried that the rigours of the journey could kill her or the baby if they try to move on. But he also knows that he must find her some food soon, or risk losing the child anyway.

His companions are unhappy with his determination to stay, and they tell him so. Neanderthal thinking and language have now progressed enough to express far more complex ideas than the *heidelbergensis* who lived here so long before: adjectives, negators, question words, qualifiers are all in their repertoire. 'No eat, no eat. Death to remain. Me go, yes?' says his companion. Ideas of the future and consequences of actions can all now be voiced, and argued, for the Neanderthal brain is large – indeed it is even larger than our own, although perhaps not in the crucial area of the frontal lobes, where our most complex reasoning is carried out. These humans are not stupid creatures; they can see a problem that matters to them and disagree about how to deal with it.

'We hunt now. Bottom valleys. Find reindeer. Come. Come yes?' The leader is determined to stick with his decision to stay in the area. Coughing again, he heads off down the slope, and comes upon a snow-covered bush. He is immediately cheered: 'Berries,' he calls out. But the smile vanishes from his face when he shakes off the snow to reveal only the shrivelled remnants of old fruit. Then suddenly, before the others have time to protest, there is flutter of movement in the snow, and the chase is on. The three heavy-set hunters have glimpsed prey, and their minds switch instantly to the task they know so well. The hunt is all-consuming, and their instant adoption of strategies to catch their victim so instinctive that they barely notice that the object of their attention is only an Arctic hare. However small, it is still food.

The men are now crashing through a sparse wood of shrunken birch trees, with the hare still out

The Neanderthal brain was larger than a modern human's. They had the ability to think through problems and a command of language.

in front. As they run through the icy air, clouds of vapour billow from their noses, which are the dominant feature of their faces. Wide and protruding, their noses are one part of their bodies that are very efficient at losing heat. The result is that during sudden exertions like this, their bodies never overheat, and so they sweat much less. That is another finely tuned adaptation to their world, because in a cold climate such as this their sweat would quickly freeze to their skin.

Briefly, the three hunters come to a halt, catching their breath, looking around them, listening for any sign of the hare. Then they are on their way again, moving rapidly down a slope after the hare. Half slipping, half leaping, the leader trips and tumbles through the undergrowth to the bottom, landing with a cry. He scrambles to his feet and looks at his hand, one finger of which is bent at a gruesome angle, clearly dislocated. Without a moment's hesitation he simply snaps it back into position, and then looks up, panting and coughing. But momentarily he smiles. His companions have caught the hare.

Later on, as the three sit around a small flame while the hare gently cooks, their faces clearly show the scars of many years of physical exertions, and their limbs reveal the bumps and twists of old broken bones. Indeed, such traces of injury are one of the characteristics of many Neanderthal fossil skeletons that have been found: they display an inordinate number of breaks and fractures, just like the kind of injuries that might be spotted in an X-ray of a modern rodeo rider. Neanderthal life was physically very demanding, and mental strength must have been just as important.

The hunter's readjustment of his dislocated finger is evidence of the tough existence the Neanderthals led. Their fossil remains reveal many broken bones during the course of their lives.

191

The Neanderthal hunters cook
the hare they have caught.

The hare has made a meagre meal, but the day is drawing to a close, and the three men are huddling down in their furs, pressed against a rocky outcrop, the flames keeping them secure for the night. In the morning they will press on. They are still concerned for the others who await them at their main camp.

The Neanderthal camp is a classic overhanging cave in a limestone cliff, with a fire flickering in the mouth. Wrapped in furs, sitting alone in the dark, is the pregnant young partner of the leader. She is using her time by securing a stone blade to a long shaft of wood. Neanderthals have now perfected the hafting of sharp stone points to their wooden spears. Inside, an old woman is checking the hair of a younger woman for lice. The close physical contact of grooming is a characteristic of early humans that has remained very strong, passed down from our most ancient ancestors. The younger woman herself is scraping the last bit of dried meat from an old piece of hide – with her teeth. Some of the others in the group are preparing for sleep, by spreading furs on the floor of the cave. The ground is filthy, littered with the detritus of Neanderthal life.

The size of this group is quite small, only eight people in all, including the hunters out in the field. This may seem like a small number, which would expose the group to danger if they lost any of their members, but in fact it is a pattern that has been found repeated wherever Neanderthal remains have been found. So it is clearly an adaptive response to the world in which they find themselves. Such small numbers mean that the ties that bind the individuals of the group are strong – they all depend on each other for survival, so the chance of major disputes between competing individuals is small. But it also means that during very hard times, such as in the depth of this ice age, what little food they can find does not have to be shared between too many mouths. This evolutionary strategy for survival in hard times, however, will one day be a factor in this species' final extinction.

Meanwhile, out in the snow, as the moon sinks below the horizon and the sun rises again on their temporary shelter, the three hunters are about to assist in the extinction of another

creature altogether. Their day is again spent tracking and scouting, as the leader grows desperate to find substantial food in this very bleak landscape. He can foresee the consequences of failure, and is becoming increasingly anxious at the thought of his leadership being challenged; and his cough has worsened. By nightfall, nothing beyond the carcass of another hare, itself the victim of the extreme cold, has turned up, and the three Neanderthals spend another uneasy night beneath the stars. The leader knows that it will take more than another rodent to counter the arguments of his companions.

Neanderthals were cave-dwellers by choice. Most of their remains suggest they lived in small groups.

193

In the bleak ice age landscape, the need to hunt for food was a daily pressure.

The following day, the ritual is repeated, and by mid afternoon they are standing on high ground, overlooking a wide valley, scanning the empty landscape for any sign of prey. But the younger hunters have decided it is pointless. They must quit the fruitless search, return to camp, and move the party to more plentiful territory. 'Sun low. No food today and day before. Move now, yes? Move now.' In the fading light of the afternoon, they turn and begin to walk away. Reluctantly, the leader has to agree, lingering to take one last look across the misty landscape before he begins to follow them.

Suddenly, from far across the valley, he registers a faint trumpeting sound: a distinctive call he has been longing to hear. 'Mammoth! Mammoth!'

A small herd of six mammoths slowly comes into view out of the evening mist. The hunters are all suddenly attentive. There is no time for argument or rebuke; no 'I told you so'. They now have a job to do: they have to form a careful plan of action, for these are creatures that cannot simply be tackled at random. At over 5 tonnes in weight, and with huge tusks 3 or 4 metres (10 to 13 feet) long, a woolly mammoth could skewer or crush an unwary Neanderthal in a moment. It is an adversary that the group might hesitate to take on. But times are hard, and this is an opportunity to get almost as much food as they could wish for. What is more, all the signs are that an attack could be successful. For all three hunters realize at once that the mammoths are moving towards the end of the valley where it narrows into a small, steep-sided ravine – the perfect spot for an ambush.

The mammoth herd, led by an old matriarch, is oblivious to the three Neanderthals looking down on them as they draw near. The men do not need to speak, as the plan forms clearly in all their minds. They run to the edge of the ravine and, as they reach it, the two younger ones hurriedly look for rocks big enough to roll down on to the animals below. With luck, one of them will injure a mammoth sufficiently for them to move close for a kill.

The leader lies down amid an array of small rocks, ready to throw them at the herd when the time is right. He acts as lookout, while the other two find large boulders near the edge of the ravine and lie on their backs, with their feet straining up against the rocks, ready to push them over at their leader's signal. 'We wait. Mammoths close. Wait.' His face is peering over the edge; the tension is palpable. With surprise on their side they stand a good chance of success, but they will only be able to strike once. It is crucial that he chooses the right moment.

(OVERLEAF) The Neanderthal hunters wait until the herd has moved on, before descending to finish off the injured mammoth.

195

Daughters of Eve

The study of human origins is like so many human sciences of the last fifty years, in that it has been transformed by the application of molecular biology to some of its central puzzles. The discovery of the structure of DNA in 1953 was one of the most important scientific milestones in history. Today the study of genes is routine, but continues to revolutionize our knowledge. In the late 1980s the revolution came to human evolution.

DNA, deoxyribonucleic acid, is the chemical that makes up our genes. It comprises just four chemical bases, strung together in two long strands that intertwine in the form of a double helix shape. A strand of DNA may contain hundreds of thousands of base pairs, and the sequence in which they line up is the genetic code that controls how every cell in our body works. When our cells divide, the lengths of DNA divide and reproduce themselves, and evolution occurs because of random mutations during that process, when a base pair mistakenly pops up in the wrong place in a new copy of the DNA. The mutations may make a gene fail or may make it perform differently, giving the organism some advantage in life. In the latter case, more of those mutations will be reproduced, and the gene will have evolved.

There is one particular type of DNA that occurs in tiny organisms inside the cell called the mitochondria, which provide energy for the cell. Our genetic material is normally provided equally by our parents, half each. But it happens that this mitochondrial DNA (mtDNA) is passed on only from our mothers, and so provides an unbroken genetic line back through our ancestry, directly inherited from our most distant mothers' mothers. Over time, mutations occur in the mtDNA, and they seem to occur at a steady frequency. So by studying the mutations in different people's mtDNA, scientists have been able to work out how closely related we all are, how far back we shared a common ancestor, and roughly when that was.

When that analysis was first done, the results were sensational, and in 1987 a team announced that they had traced the common ancestor of all humans alive on Earth to an individual who had lived in Africa over 200,000 years ago. She was dubbed the African Eve, and her notional existence confirmed the then growing belief that modern humans had evolved after that time in Africa, and that a wave of them had subsequently swept across the globe, replacing all the more ancient hominid lines that were already established in the Middle East, Asia and Europe. *Homo erectus* in the east and *Homo neanderthalensis* in the north were all eclipsed by the new smarter *Homo sapiens*. There are still a few scientists who do not accept this scenario, but the 'Out of Africa' hypothesis is unquestionably the view of our history that is most widely agreed. In addition, it is clear that the genetic variation between all humans alive today is tiny. In fact, two lowland gorillas living next door to each other in central Africa may have more differences in their DNA than would two human races from opposite sides of the globe. We come from a very tightly knit evolutionary family.

Recent studies have refined the original mtDNA work, and pushed the date of the common ancestor to modern humans back even further, but the origin remains firmly in Africa, so 'Out of Africa' still stands. And newer work on the DNA found in the Y-chromosome (the stretch of DNA that is always passed on from the males to their sons) of the cell has arrived at an African Adam some 200,000 years ago also.

More still has been done with mtDNA studies. Recent work by Professor Bryan Sykes at the University of Oxford tracked the lineages of 95 per cent of all Europeans living today to seven different female lines who lived between 10,000 and 40,000 years ago. Sykes has dubbed these the Seven Daughters of Eve, for all of them of course share the ultimate origin of the African Eve.

Professor Sykes got his inspiration for the research from a story he had read as a boy which told him that all the hamsters alive in the world could be traced back to one pregnant female found in the desert of Syria in 1930. Years later he applied the same reasoning to a study of mitochondrial DNA. By way of separating the different ancestral lines, he gives the women

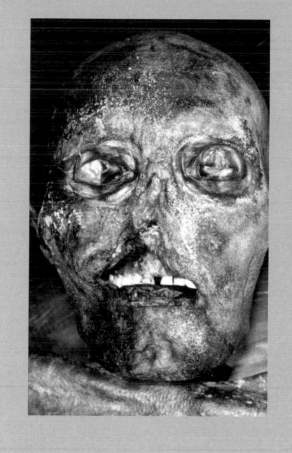

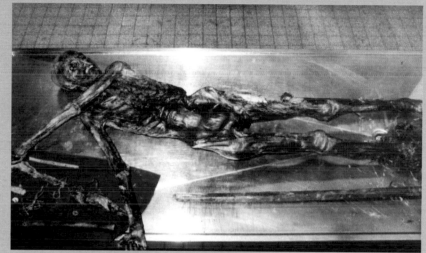

(LEFT AND ABOVE) In 1991 a frozen body was found high in the Italian Alps. It turned out to be that of a prehistoric hunter, from 5,500 years ago. Analysis of DNA from the remains of the man enabled scientists to trace his descendants amongst samples already held in their laboratory. This direct genetic connection with a prehistoric ancestor prompted Professor Bryan Sykes to undertake a study of the genetic origins of all Europeans.

fictional names. The furthest back is Ursula, stemming from the region of Greece 45,000 years ago, but whose descendants are now spread throughout Europe. Xenia was from the Caucasus Mountains 25,000 years ago, and her line spread across Europe and eventually into North America. From 17,000 years ago the descendants of Tara travelled from Tuscany on into northern Europe and across the English Channel to Britain. Valda, from Spain between 17,000 and 13,000 years ago, gave rise to a line that spread to Finland and Norway. Helena is the 'mother' of some 47 per cent of Europeans, and her line

began in the Pyrenees 12,000 years ago, right at the end of the last great glaciation of the ice age. Katrine stems from the area of Venice, 10,000 years ago, and most of her descendants now live in the Alps. Finally, the origin of Jasmine is in Syria around the same time, and her descendants spread throughout Europe, perhaps bringing agriculture as they travelled.

Of course the precise starting point of each of these lines will never be known, and there has even been a recent reassessment of the research to arrive at eleven lines. But the fundamental finding that most of us are born of ancestors

who were here at the time of the Cro-Magnons is of great significance. It has long been believed that the origins of agriculture and civilization stemmed from waves of immigration from the Middle East, with farmers bringing their ideas and taking over the population at the same time. Instead, it now seems that if the ideas indeed did come from the Middle East they were passed on to the original inhabitants of the land to use. Or perhaps the inspiration that enabled Europeans to build their civilizations even emerged locally, from the creative minds of the people who had come through the ice age.

Neanderthals made crude
clothing from animal skins.

For the mammoths, this is one of many familiar routes that the
matriarch chooses as they head south in search of warmer climes,
but she is becoming edgy as they enter the narrow confines of the
ravine. Above them, the three hunters hardly dare to breathe
for fear of letting this opportunity slip through their hands.
But as the animals are almost there, the leader lets slip a
small cough. His companions look at each other in alarm.
For a brief moment, time seems to stop. At first the
mammoths do not seem to have heard the tell-tale noise,
but it is only a few seconds before they react – 30 tonnes
of chaos breaks out. The matriarch repeatedly screeches
in alarm, while the rest of the herd, hemmed in by the
narrow rock walls and confused as to what has
happened, begin to turn around and collide with
each other in the ensuing panic.

But the Neanderthal leader holds his nerve.
Getting quickly to his feet, he glances from the
boulders to the herd below, trying to judge again the
moment to strike. By now the matriarch is beginning
to lead the herd back out of the ravine, and he is faced
with an erratic moving target, but he knows that he has
no choice but to attack now, or lose the opportunity for
ever. He turns and gestures sharply to his companions,
and with a concerted heave each launches his boulder
over the edge of the ravine and into space.

Again there is a moment that seems to last for ever
as they wait for the effect of the attack to become clear;
and then celebration: one of the large boulders has struck
a mature female mammoth on the hip. It screeches in pain and
then collapses on to its haunches. Immediately the hunters begin
to pelt it with smaller rocks, until it becomes dazed and panicked.
It irrevocably damages its broken hip by thrashing around in vain
attempts to get to its feet and flee. The Neanderthals stop the
onslaught. The mammoth is not dead, but they know that they
can afford to wait. Time will be their weapon now.

And as the deepening gloom of evening bears down on them, the leader raps out an instruction to his fellows: 'Fire!' The rest of the mammoth herd have fled from the valley, and it is time for the hunters to finish their work. One of his companions bends to the ground and, with flint and dry wood, soon has a small blaze aglow. The three men clamber down the ravine, with the leader brandishing a flaming torch as they approach the exhausted mammoth. While he distracts the terrified animal with the threat of fire, the others carefully avoid the flailing tusks and stab it repeatedly in the neck and flanks with their long stabbing spears. Mercifully, the kill is over quickly, as one of the spear thrusts succeeds in piercing the animal's main artery. The Neanderthals are jubilant.

The three hunters return to their base camp, and sit round the fire with the rest of the group, enjoying the spoils. The leader, still coughing, is cutting off pieces of meat with a sharpened flake of stone, while his young female partner sits by his side grooming him. The two young hunters have now relaxed, all criticism of their leader forgotten. One of them is humming quietly to himself, as he chews, while the other eats greedily, with a piece of meat in both hands. For the leader, the successful hunt means the end of his anxiety in the short term. The meat that they do not eat now can be kept for a long time in the freezing snow, so they have plenty of food to last them until long after the birth of his child. When that is over, the group will be able to move on to better land. He is happy.

Suddenly the greedy young hunter gulps and chokes. The others turn to look at him in alarm, but after several moments of panic, with his eyes

The leader uses a scraper to remove flesh from a mammoth skin. The Neanderthals made tools for specific purposes.

Physical grooming was still an occasional part of the Neanderthal behaviour.

staring, and his face bulging and red, the offending lump of meat spews out of his windpipe and flies across the camp, striking another member of the group in the eye. The group bursts into fits of laughter, which echo out of the overhanging cave and down into the valley below. Neanderthals are creatures who have time in their lives for more than simply the process of survival.

Despite the obvious differences between us and them, there is a lot about Neanderthal behaviour that would have been similar to our own: their joy at being reunited, or their contentment at feeling warm and well fed. They would have had an awareness of themselves as living beings, and their place in their world; they would have understood what is normal, what is routine and what is unexpected. They would have laughed at themselves, and enjoyed a social life for its own sake. For many thousands of generations they did little with this intellectual power, for their world was still rooted in the immediate reality of their daily lives. But much later, near the end of their time on Earth, we will see that their potential for creativity and imagination was far greater than perhaps they themselves ever realized.

Although the Neanderthals were pushed to the limit by the ice age, they were supremely well adapted to their world, and were destined to survive the harshness of the European climate for a further 100,000 years. Meanwhile, at the same time as they enjoyed their heyday in the north, in Africa their hominid cousins were experiencing climatic hardship of a very different kind. But in so doing they set the stage for the eventual domination of all other species by *Homo sapiens*.

The large Neanderthal brain almost certainly allowed them moments of relaxation and humour, this time caused by the greed of the young hunter.

Just how close were the Neanderthals and *Homo sapiens*?

The Neanderthals dominated Europe for over 200,000 years, during some of its harshest and most testing extremes of climate. They had large brains, lived in tight-knit communities, and were capable of detailed communication and planning. They could so easily have gone on to live for generations up to the present day. But within 10,000 years of the arrival of modern humans in their midst – the mere blink of an eye in evolutionary terms – they were no more. Or were they? Ten thousand years, or 500 generations, is a very long time in terms of human lifespan. If modern humans co-existed for so long with creatures that were so close to them in so many physical ways, is it credible that they did not interbreed? That question has remained high on the list of puzzles for palaeoanthropologists ever since the Neanderthals were discovered in the Feldhofer Cave in the Neander Valley near Dusseldorf in Germany in 1856. Were they our direct ancestors?

Neanderthals have suffered from a bad image ever since their discovery. Their existence became known exactly at the time that Darwin's theory of evolution by natural selection was being published for the first time, and when the debate over our origins was at its most vocal. Victorian society was keen to see humans as the pinnacle of evolution, and the shock of another prehistoric species coming along with worrying similarities to modern people was enough to consign the Neanderthals to a century of general abuse. For the best part of a hundred years pictures based on scientific study of Neanderthal bones portray the man as a variant on a hairy, stooping, weapon-wielding thug.

The remains of almost 500 individual Neanderthals have now been discovered, ranging from as far afield as the Uzbekistan mountains near Samarkand, through the Middle East and central Europe to the tip of the Iberian peninsula. One such find in the 1960s, that of a burial site at Shanidar in Iraq, revealed pollen from spring flowers in the grave of three Neanderthals, and prompted a new view of the hominids, appropriate to the time, suggesting that they were in fact gentle flower people. It turns out that the pollen find may well have been due to contamination, and so the nature of any burial activity is still in doubt, but at least the Neanderthals had gained a better image, and by and large they have been treated with a little more sympathy in recent years.

Over the years, as more and more different hominid species have emerged from prehistory, so the question of the exact path of our ancestry has become more intriguing. Whether or not the Neanderthals were our direct ancestors has lain at the centre of hot scientific debate. The physical differences between our species – the brow-ridge, the nose,

The skeleton of a Neanderthal, found at Kebara in Israel.

the lack of a chin, the sloping forehead, the squat and differently proportioned limbs – all suggested a different line of descent from the modern humans who co-existed with them in Europe. Then in 1997 came a remarkable piece of scientific work that seemed to have decided the issue. In a breakthrough reminiscent of the fictional achievements of *Jurassic Park*, a team from Munich University led by Svante Pääbo succeeded in extracting viable DNA from a Neanderthal fossil bone. In fact they took it from the first specimen discovered.

Scientists had been trying for years to get Neanderthal DNA, but the task is supremely difficult, as the strands of the double helix are fragile and easily destroyed over time. But the Feldhofer Cave sample is from a relatively recent Neanderthal, so the bone has not yet fully mineralized to stone, and also the low temperature inside the cave may have helped to preserve the DNA. Pääbo and his colleagues multiplied up the tiny quantity of genetic material they had isolated, and sequenced it to try to identify a gene that they could compare with known human genes.

They managed to get a length of 378 base pairs (the fundamental building blocks of DNA), which was enough to find a match with a human gene, although it is a tiny length compared to the many thousands of base pairs that make up a complete human gene. But when they compared the two strands they found a very clear pattern. Across all human populations there are always natural variations in the genes, caused by random mutations. In this stretch of the genome there are normally about eight differences seen between modern humans. However, the Neanderthal DNA

differed in twenty-seven places from the modern human gene, far beyond the range of *Homo sapiens*. By contrast, chimpanzees show up fifty-five differences with the human gene, so the research suggested that Neanderthals were somewhere between the two on the tree of life. In fact the calculations suggest that our line of descent split away from the ancestors of the Neanderthals around 650,000 years ago.

The result has since been confirmed by testing two other samples of Neanderthal DNA: a fossil from a cave in Croatia, and a fossil rib of a Neanderthal child found in the Caucasus. The Neanderthal genes are not found in modern humans. Of course it is possible that one day a gene will be extracted that does match, but for now it seems that we did not interbreed – at least not successfully. But there is a tantalizing piece of evidence of a very different kind. At Lagar Velho in Portugal, near the coast on the western tip of Europe, the point that would have been the last to be reached by the advancing

modern humans, a skeleton of a four-year-old child has been uncovered, dating from around 25,000 years ago. This was a time long after the last Neanderthal is known to have lived. The skeleton was partly coated in red ochre, and a shell bead lay near it, all signs of modern human activity. It had the pronounced chin and teeth of a modern human but, remarkably, it had very thick bones, like those of a Neanderthal, and the proportion of the upper and lower bones of each limb was like that of a Neanderthal, opposite to that of a modern human. In other words it seems like a hybrid.

The interpretation is controversial but, if correct, the features could be the product of interbreeding between the species. It may be that in the long term no such descendants survived to bequeath us their genes, but it leaves open the possibility that contact between the Neanderthals and the people who took over their world may have been more intimate after all.

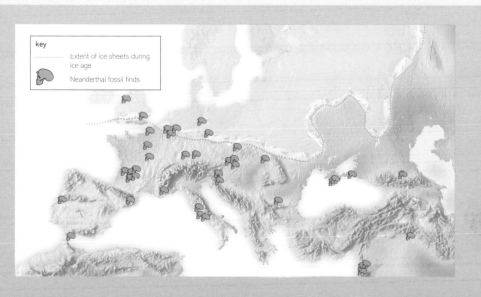

key

········· Extent of ice sheets during ice age

Neanderthal fossil finds

(LEFT) *Homo Neanderthalis* dominated Europe throughout the most intense period of the ice age.

A *Homo sapiens* woman scratches at the parched ground in an attempt to find roots or a trace of water.

AFRICAN HARDSHIP

East Africa, 150,000 years ago. A woman, covered in a fine layer of dust, is digging a hole in the sandy soil with a digging stick. She works down a few feet, and then pauses and moves on, to start another. Behind her are dozens of these holes. She is digging patiently for water along the dried-up bed of a river that once flowed through the valley. She is also hoping to turn up the odd root or tuber, because these and the remaining pockets of moisture in the river are the only sources of water she can rely on. She is not optimistic, but she has to persevere, as she desperately needs water to allow her to produce milk for her infant child.

As she wends her way along the length of the dried river bed, she passes the skeletons and rotting remains of animals that have died on its banks: gazelle, elephant and crocodile. This is drought in its most extreme form, and it has been part of her life since she can remember. The ice caps at the poles have grown so large that much of the Earth's water is now trapped in ice-sheets and glaciers. Less moisture is being drawn into the atmosphere, and so, globally, there is much less rain. And this is most noticeably felt in sub-Saharan Africa, where the population of hominids is experiencing hardship like none that their ancestors have ever faced. Along the side of the creek, just shaded from the direct heat, a group sits huddled together out of the sun. Flies play about their faces with impunity; all of the group are too weak to bother brushing them away. The woman gives up her fruitless digging for water, and returns to the others. As she approaches, the others look up at her with pity. An older woman gets to her feet, and hands her the body of her lifeless child.

Physically, these early *Homo sapiens* were almost indistinguishable from us.

These people are the African descendants of the descendants of *Homo ergaster*. While *heidelbergensis* had flourished in the north, something very like it had evolved in sub-Saharan Africa, known sometimes as Kabwe Man after the town in Zambia where the fossils were found. But in turn, Kabwe Man and his cousins had given way to a new hominid line: the early *Homo sapiens* – the very first anatomically modern human beings, who appeared around 150,000 years ago. Physically, these early *Homo sapiens* were almost indistinguishable from us. Virtually gone was the heavy brow-ridge; the face was flatter, the small nose was there, and the chin clearly formed, and above all a high forehead sweeping up to form a cranium that housed a large brain, which was virtually the same size as ours. But nowhere in the fossil record are any signs of the human creativity or cultural behaviour that mark out the special nature of humanity. What is clear is that these creatures' survival was ultimately tested by the extreme dryness of the climate, and the test drove them almost to extinction.

At the stage in their evolution that our story has found them, it is thought that the population of *Homo sapiens* in Africa was reduced

to perhaps a few tens of thousands, about the same number as orang-utans alive in the world today – an endangered species. The evidence for this, remarkably, comes from studying our genes. By looking at mutations in modern human DNA it is possible to work out how long ago we shared common human ancestors, and how widely we have spread from that time, and it seems that our species faced what is called a 'genetic bottleneck' out of which we all emerged. There is no certainty as to the cause of this evolutionary pressure-point, but it is very possible that it is linked to the extreme climate change around the glacial maximum of 150,000 years ago.

Across the continent of Africa, small populations of early *Homo sapiens* struggled through the arid conditions. Some did not make it, others did. Perhaps, on the margins, some were fortunate enough to have lived in local areas that provided water, vegetation and game, and these people carried on unaffected; but for many others the numbers in their small groups dwindled dangerously low. Yet the effect of that extreme climate pressure on these first humans may have been to create the very attributes that make us so successful today. This was like the process of evolution turned up to maximum speed, because when a small population is under pressure only the very fittest survive, and in drought-ridden prehistoric Africa, fitness meant living by their wits. The difference between life and death could come down simply to a good idea.

(OPPOSITE) The earliest *Homo sapiens* evolved in Africa in an era of extensive drought.

The difference between life and death could come down simply to a good idea.

SURVIVORS

Far on from the huddled group of dying people, over a mountain range, across valleys, past other dried-up rivers, and on through many generations of time, another tiny group of humans is walking, foraging as they go, but clearly on a journey. They are a couple and their young daughter, and they are patently exhausted from a morning of toil. But the woman approaches a very dry-looking tree, to dig round one side of the base, until she unearths a round white

Homo sapiens

Who discovered *Homo sapiens*?

In 1868, a geologist called Louis Lartet and a banker called Henry Christy discovered the skeletons of some anatomically modern people in the Cro-Magnon rock shelter near the village of Les Eysies in south-west France, dating from about 25,000 years ago. The name Cro-Magnon came to be used for all the *Homo sapiens* who populated Europe after the Neanderthals, and who created the fabulous cave paintings of prehistory. But in 1967 the great Kenyan fossil hunter, Kamoya Kimeu, found a skull at Kibish in the Omo Basin of Ethiopia, and this is probably the best candidate for the earliest hominid with the features of a modern human.

Where did *Homo sapiens* live?

It is not precisely clear where anatomically modern humans first emerged, but East Africa is thought to be the most likely place. Studies of our own DNA suggest a modern origin of humans in Africa, from where they spread (see the feature on pages 198–9). Skulls similar to Omo have been found in Israel from a slightly later date, and fragments of modern human fossils have been found along with more advanced tools in South Africa also from the same period. Together this suggests that *Homo sapiens* moved out of East Africa quite soon. It is not certain by which route, but they soon moved into Asia and Europe, replacing the archaic creatures who had lived there.

When did *Homo sapiens* live?

The Omo skull itself cannot be precisely dated, but shells found in the same layer of sediment as the skull have been dated to 130,000 years ago. Extreme fluctuations in the climate could well have created the evolutionary pressure that drove the emergence of modern humans. Genetic studies suggest that the population of our direct ancestors was severely reduced around 150,000 to 100,000 years ago, which is a time that coincides with an intense advance of the ice age, drawing water from the atmosphere and causing severe droughts in Africa. In such extreme circumstances only the fittest survive and, in the case of our ancestors, fitness was cleverness. The most creative people lived.

What did *Homo sapiens* look like?

The Omo Man's skeleton showed that he was sturdy but taller and lighter than the Neanderthals, had a high forehead, a pronounced chin and modern-sized teeth. He had a brain the size of our own. He still retains some archaic features, such as a slightly heavy brow-ridge, but Omo Man is clearly of the same line as we are. The Cro-Magnon had higher domed skulls, with very small brow-ridges, and prominent chins. They were tall, long-legged and muscular, and to all intents were identical to us today. Interestingly, while early Cro-Magnon were tall and slim, later finds tend to be shorter and more sturdy, suggesting that they had adapted to the colder European climate.

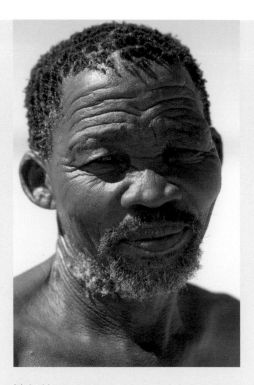

Male *Homo sapiens.*

How would *Homo sapiens* have lived?

In southern Africa 100,000 years ago, there is fragmentary evidence that early *Homo sapiens* had already evolved its creativity: there are more advanced tools, carved markings on bone, and signs of the use of red ochre as decoration. But evidence for a full picture of early human life has been found in Europe only after about 40,000 years ago. The Cro-Magnon people of France lived in larger settlements than the Neanderthals. They traded stone, beads and shells over huge distances, and they moved camp to follow the seasons. They built up a sophisticated toolkit of stone, bone, ivory and wood. Above all they left behind spectacular paintings on their cave walls (see the feature on pages 214–5), which reveal a sophisticated sense of ritual and spiritual belief.

object and draws it out. It is a very large ostrich egg, but it is not food for her family. She removes a plug of grass stuffed into a small hole, raises it to her lips and drinks: water. This is something that she and her partner placed there weeks ago, perhaps even months, when there was some rain. They knew that one day they would be passing this way again, and when they did, this water might be just what they needed.

A simple but life-saving idea such as this would have marked the survivors out from those whose line came to an end, but it also illustrates what was special about the humans that survived. This was not simply the spark of lateral thinking needed to use an ostrich egg for a very different purpose. This was forward planning. They had an ability to think of what might happen in the future, and to work out a way of dealing with it. When the climate eventually changed for the better, if indeed that was the reason for the pressure on the species, the human ancestors who came through the bottleneck were the ones who were fittest not just physically,

The *Homo sapiens* family undertake their journey knowing that there are supplies of water along the way.

but mentally. They were the ones who could think their way out of the crushing circumstances they were in. They were the ones who had developed what we would call an imagination. And the small population size meant that this mental attribute very quickly, in evolutionary terms, became a feature of the human population.

As the couple continue their journey, the woman begins to lag behind. The man turns and chides her, clearly wanting her to catch up. She in turn rebukes him with a short stream of angry words that we would not recognize. But words they are, for these survivors of the climatic squeeze on the planet have developed the ability to share their imagination, their plans and their point of view with others. Around this time, a little over 100,000 years ago, modern humans have begun to master the art of language, with a subtlety far beyond the Neanderthals' communication of needs, actions and immediate concerns. Human imagination has brought with it an ability to think far outside their immediate circumstances, to think in metaphor and analogy, and the use of language enables humans to use symbolic expression. It enables them to work with a wider range of other humans than ever before.

With a shake of the head, the man is silent, and the trio resume their journey. They have been walking for the best part of a day in search of something that will guarantee their survival: not food or water, but a mate for their daughter. Arriving at an open sandflat, they find another, larger, party of humans waiting for them, and for a moment the two groups eye each other warily, weighing up the situation. Finally the leader of the larger group breaks the tension, stepping forward in greeting and speaking to the new arrival. The other man steps near and gestures for the girl to come forward, and in turn the leader of the large group calls for a young boy to step out.

The early *Homo sapiens* strengthened their gene pool by forming alliances with neighbouring groups.

This is perhaps how a simple union between neighbouring family groups might be arranged. But whatever the ceremonial procedure, the advantages of such a union are clear to both sides. Each will now have allies to rely on, and so will stand more chance of survival when times become hard again, as both men know they will. As the meeting carries on into the evening, the men converse and agree the terms, perhaps promises of help, that will be to their mutual advantage. Language has become the means by which whole groups can create and share a web of culture; it is a kind of social glue. And at the most primitive level, this ability to share information and common experience, to share the future with another group, and to widen the immediate family, means that the species can exchange more genes, more quickly, and become ever stronger as a result.

So the stage is set for the final epic moments in the human story. To the north in Western Europe and in the Middle East the Neanderthals were the end stage of evolutionary adaptation to the harsher colder climate. To the south in the heat of Africa, it was the modern humans. We will never know the precise journey that was taken but, over the 100,000 years that followed the emergence of anatomically modern humans in Africa, armed with their sophisticated intelligence and ability to adapt to any environment, they moved across the globe, and reached almost every continent. The effect on the populations of archaic humans that already existed in those territories was perhaps inevitable. In the Far East, pockets of *Homo erectus*, the longest surviving species of *Homo* ever to have lived, were still alive as late as 50,000 years ago. Now of course they are no more. But it is in Europe that the flowering of *Homo sapiens* success as a species is most graphically displayed.

CREATIVE TAKE-OVER

Night-time in southern France, 30,000 years ago. A man is busy making a lamp, twisting a piece of animal sinew round using his teeth to make a wick. He pours some fat into a hollowed flat stone, and uses an ember from a campfire to ignite it. He turns and enters a narrow passage in the cliff face behind him, and begins to walk deep

(OPPOSITE) Cave painting of bison and lions or panthers, from la Grotte de Chauvet, in France.

into a cave system. Led by the flickering flame, his shadows rise and fall against the walls of rock, as he walks, crawls and climbs for as much as half an hour to reach a vast cavern deep within. There he pauses, and stares around him at walls adorned with paintings of extraordinary beauty. Some of these are his own work. Some of them were created by his ancestors, his family, or his fellows. For him, the images of animals, hunters, people and geometric patterns are of immense significance. Slowly, from within his clothing, he draws out a rolled-up package containing a dark pigment. He takes some into his mouth, raises his right hand against the wall of the cave and sprays the paint over his spread-out fingers. Gently lowering his hand, he sees its shape perfectly imprinted on the rock before him. He is satisfied.

But there we will leave him. Because, although we know that such an action was carried out many times during the long years that prehistoric humans occupied this part of the world, we will never know why men or women like these painted their caves. We will never know the beliefs that urged them to go to such lengths to create art. We will never know the nature of any ceremonies that were central to their work. All of our interpretation of the cave paintings of southern Europe can only be speculation, however well informed. What we do know is that all across this region at this time, thousands of images were painted, depicting the natural world in extraordinary, imaginative and beautiful detail. Indeed, the reason why they were painted is largely unimportant. The key is that these people chose to take time from the rigours of physical survival to practise a newly evolved skill that they believed was important to them. We can really only marvel at this great explosion of creativity that occurred among those human ancestors, and recognize it as evidence that their minds had reached a level of advancement that is indistinguishable from our own. Indeed, if a prehistoric human baby could be plucked from the cave painters of southern France and brought up alongside a modern child, there is no reason why it would not reach the very highest levels of modern education and cultural sophistication that our most successful offspring achieve today.

Images from a lost world

The 'Lady of Brassempouy'.

The Ardèche Gorge is in a region of south-eastern France that is a veritable heaven for potholers. Long twisting hollows that narrow to the width of a person, then open to a dark echoing void, only to end in shafts that plunge perilously away in the darkness – all these are a source of challenge to adventurers. But for many years they have also provided a barrier to the discovery of the contents of some of this subterranean world. Only the most daring would explore the labyrinthine tunnels.

In December 1994, Jean-Marie Chauvet and two colleagues were spending a Sunday doing just that, and were searching for the source of a draught of cool air that had come through a pile of boulders. They had used a rope ladder to descend into a cavern, when they saw what is one of the artistic wonders of the world. The rock of the cave glittered with mineral deposits, reflecting the light of their torches, and the floor was littered with the bones of bears. But all around them were paintings in red ochre, black charcoal and white pigment. On the walls were over 300 drawings of animals: lions, buffalo, deer and woolly rhinoceros, hunting in packs or running in herds. It is one of the finest examples of prehistoric cave art in the world, and Jean-Marie is proud to have had it named after him: la Grotte de Chauvet.

The first signs of prehistoric cave art were probably seen by French and Spanish shepherds many years before they became known for what they were, but in the late 1860s and the 1870s notes appear in the diaries of scholars who wondered at the remarkable images they had stumbled across, but took them no further. Indeed, there is even a tantalizing reference to fantastic paintings in a cave in the Ardèche. But when the news of such finds was eventually reported, the archaeological establishment found it hard to accept that prehistoric people could be responsible for the paintings that were found. The first published discovery of Palaeolithic art, engravings on the walls of a cave called Chabot in France in 1878, was dismissed. Likewise, the discovery of spectacular paintings in the Spanish cave of Altamira in 1879 was quickly put down to fraud by the leading academic lights of the day. It remained under suspicion for over a decade, but has all along been one of the treasures of prehistoric human art, famed for a ceiling over 18 metres (nearly 60 feet) long, adorned by the rich colours of scores of paintings of bison.

Evidence for early human expressions of art is always highly controversial, disputed at the worst of times, and subject to widely different interpretation at the best. There is no agreement as to when, why or even how our ancestors began to express themselves artistically. At one extreme there is a claim that two and a half million years ago the australopithecines demonstrated some awareness by collecting a stone and transporting it some 32 kilometres (20 miles) because its natural wear resembles that of a hominid face. At the other extreme is the argument that our latent artistic expression only truly emerged in the last 50,000 years with the modern humans of western Europe, the Cro-Magnons. The truth is probably somewhere in between. Certainly it is unwise to assume that just because most of the cave paintings date from an era around 15,000 to 20,000 years ago, then that is when such art forms began. Indeed, when Chauvet was dated it turned out to be an astonishing 33,000 years old (although that is disputed, of course), and yet its art is some of the most creative and sophisticated ever found. Some scholars interpret the images of many rhinoceros as being a herd drawn in perspective. Clearly a skill such as that did not simply emerge full-blown one prehistoric morning.

The use of red ochre by early humans has left tantalizing clues. A South African hominid site from 800,000 years ago turned up bits of ochre that appeared to have been brought there, and in India an ochre pebble, marked with lines, may have been used in the manner of a crayon at a 200,000-year-old site. Engravings and carvings have been dated from an early era: at Klasies River in South Africa, a well-established early *Homo sapiens* site from 100,000 years ago, a bone marked with criss-cross lines suggests an expression of symbolic thought. Beads and pierced shells also date from a similar time. But there is clearly an explosion of artistic prowess around 40,000 years ago. The tools that the people were using became much more sophisticated, with exquisitely carved bone needles and hooks. Tiny figurines of immense beauty, despite their simplicity, are found from more than 30,000 years ago. They are minute female statues known as 'Venus' figures. Perhaps the most remarkable is the 'Lady of Brassempouy', a tiny female head, carved from mammoth ivory, with perfectly proportioned nose, cheeks and

eyes, and carefully crafted long braided hair. She dates from 25,000 years ago, and was found among the detritus on a cave floor.

Interpretation of the meaning of Palaeolithic art is even more rife with disagreement. The exaggerated physical features of some of the Venus figurines clearly suggest a use as fertility symbols. But other art is not so straightforward. The most obvious explanation is that the people were concerned on a daily basis with the success of their hunting, and the cave walls of Altamira, Chauvet, Lascaux and many, many more clearly represent the actions of the chase, with spears sometimes penetrating the animals' sides, and creatures portrayed at the moment of death. But the caves are also filled with other symbols, such as patterns of grids and squares, and regular dots. One group of academics has suggested that these symbols are very similar to those experienced by people today when they

enter a state of trance, and they have noted similarities with the art of present-day bushmen who also describe their visions in a trance. These scientists argue that perhaps some of the cave paintings represent the work of prehistoric shamans, in a self-induced trance, attempting to reach into a spirit world.

And what of the very simple image that is seen in so many of the caves – that of the outline of a human hand? Was that symbolic, or was it just the sign of someone, often a child, simply saying 'I was here'? Of course we will never know. But if one ever gets the chance to see these remarkable caves, it is worth sometimes looking away from the magnificent wall paintings and down to the floor, where still preserved in the petrified mud are the footprints of children and adults who once walked there. They were people who had minds as great as our own, but whose thoughts were simply in another time.

(FAR LEFT) Painting of a bull, from Lascaux cave in France.

(LEFT) Silhouetted hand from 20,000BC, in Peche Merle in southern France. It was created by blowing a sooty pigment over the hand pressed against the cave wall.

EXTINCTION

There is a postscript. The art and adornments of modern humans
also provide a remarkable insight into their way of life. Studies of
their domestic remains, their stone tools, the beads and shells that
they used to create necklaces or pendants, and the fine bone needles
they used to stitch their clothing, have revealed an intricate map of
the travels that they undertook. Shells from the coast of Spain are
found in the remains of settlements in the mountains of central
France, beads from central Europe are found on the Atlantic coast,
seeds of lowland plants are found in upland caves. Clearly these
people built up a web of trade and exchange throughout Europe,
meeting other groups, exchanging goods and at the same time
widening their gene pool, an evolutionary strategy for success.

When the first modern humans reached into
Europe, they began to co-exist alongside the
Neanderthals, who by contrast left no evidence of
trade or travel. All of their materials were
obtained locally. They had dominated the land
for over 200,000 years, and their large brains
must have had great ingenuity, to adapt to the
succession of climatic and environmental
changes that occurred throughout that
era. Yet in all that time the
Neanderthals created no art, nor left
any firm trace of imagination. There
are signs that some of them buried
their dead, but there is no evidence of
any ritual associated with that, and it
could have been simply a means of
cleanly disposing of a corpse, rather
than an expression of belief in an
afterlife. But then, perhaps 500
generations after the time that *Homo
sapiens* first entered their world, the
Neanderthals too began to leave

traces of works of art. Simple tooth pendants have been found in French caves among the layers left behind from Neanderthal occupation. These are clearly objects of adornment, with no practical purpose other than display. The puzzle that is left for archaeologists to resolve, but which possibly never will be, is whether the Neanderthals had themselves begun to show the imaginative leaps that could have led them to greater sophistication and perhaps survival, or whether they were simply copying the practices that they had observed and realized were valuable to their ever more powerful neighbours.

Whichever it was, it was not enough to prevent the modern human domination of Europe by 30,000 years ago. The human ability to network across large distances, along with their creative ability, meant that they could adapt to almost any climate or environmental change, and there were many fluctuations in the climate throughout the period up to the end of the last ice age. It is unlikely that there was any great violent take-over of the Neanderthals, but rather that the moderns simply out-competed them for resources in times of both plenty and harshness. Living in small groups, the Neanderthal population would have become a collection of isolated pockets. And it is impossible to know what the Neanderthals thought of their new neighbours – in some ways quite like them but in others very different. But with their far-reaching networks and strange customs, and with so many more of them arriving with each new generation, we can only assume that they seemed quite terrifying.

There is a saying in evolution that you do not have to fail to become extinct; you just have to succeed a little less often. In the end, the last Neanderthal died, some time around 28,000 years ago, perhaps just 1,500 generations before our time. And when that moment came, we were alone. For the first time in over six million years there was only one species of human on the planet.

Neanderthals lived alongside *Homo sapiens* for over 500 generations, but finally were out-competed by the newcomers.

Conclusion

We have reached the end of our journey and, having traced the path from australopithecine to human, we can look at ourselves with new eyes and see how our bodies and minds have been shaped by the powerful forces of evolution. We can also see how the formidable intelligence, language skills and tool-making techniques that first emerged in our ancestors have allowed us to escape from those evolutionary forces so that we are no longer at the mercy of nature. Instead of being forced to adapt to the environment, we, as modern humans, have the capacity to adapt the environment to suit us.

Our complex culture allows us to build on the insights and inventions of previous generations so that, in less than a hundred years, we were able to go from the first powered flight to sending rockets to the moon. The invention of the telephone, the internet and e-mail allows us to communicate with people over the entire planet with ease, people we may never set eyes on in person. We can share ideas not only through talking to each other, but through books, radio and television. We control our world to an extent never before seen on the planet, but it is clear that our capacity to do so rests squarely on the abilities that evolution bred into us, all of which stem from the simple act of standing on two feet instead of four.

This adaptation allowed our ancestors to move beyond the forests, into new, challenging habitats. But this alone was not enough. Over the next million years, these creatures gained the ingenuity and flexibility to survive and, with the invention of stone tools, to overcome their natural limitations. Caring for vulnerable offspring and sharing food and songs were the beginnings of empathy and love. But it wasn't until *Homo sapiens* emerged that we were able to explore imagined worlds that were made real through paintings and ritual, through culture. It should also be clear that this was all a matter of chance. There was nothing inevitable about our evolution – we have made it here by a series of lucky accidents. The hominid family has evolved like every other animal group on Earth; there have been periods when new species have burst forth rapidly in response to environmental change, times when evolution has experimented with different ways of being hominid. Some lines went extinct while others prospered, the fate of each species hanging in the balance as the climate and environment changed erratically over time. This resulted in a human family tree that is thick and bushy, with many branches leading off from it, each of which tells an interesting story in its own right, even if those branches have no link to our own species.

The most remarkable thing of all is that today we find ourselves alone on the planet – we no longer have *afarensis*, *boisei* and the Neanderthals to show us other ways of being a hominid, and maybe our complex capacities and our solitude are linked. Perhaps the cultural niche we occupy, one that enables us to live in every habitat on the planet from the high Arctic to the heart of the desert, leaves no room for another species. Today, having spent some time seeing how our ancestors lived and what they were like, we can feel sadness and regret that they no longer share the planet with us, that we have no remaining links with the rest of the human family tree.

We have all played the game of 'what-if': 'What if I hadn't gone to that party? I would have never met my future partner.' 'What if I had decided to take this job instead of that one?' 'What if I had decided to make the effort to learn Spanish?' Would our lives have taken an entirely different path? Would we have been completely different people? Chances are, the answer is yes. And the same is true for the lives of our ancestors. What if the creation of the Himalayas had never taken place? Would there be any hominids at all? Would a creature like *afarensis* ever have evolved if there was no need to travel efficiently on two legs? Would apes still rule the vast forests of Africa? It could so easily have been that way.

And what if there had been no ice ages, no periods of cooling that helped create the vast savannahs? Without the creation of new habitats, the early australopithecines would not have evolved into so many different species. There would have been no *Homo habilis* or *ergaster*. No pressure to evolve big brains or invent stone tools. What if climate change had, in fact, favoured animals like *boisei* and it was *ergaster* that went extinct? Would australopithecines now dominate the planet? Could *boisei* have evolved language or culture? Would there be any towns and cities, airports and hospitals? Perhaps not.

It is humbling to think that, despite our intelligence and ingenuity, our evolution has depended so heavily on a succession of chance events; a slightly larger fluctuation in the Earth's temperature or a greater tilt in the angle of the Earth's rotation and we may never have evolved at all.

We have been on a journey to visit our ancestors and tell the story of our evolution, but the story we have told is by no means complete. Indeed, it is only one of many possible tales there for the telling. There are still many gaps in our knowledge, many branches on our family tree that are still to be found. There are thousands of fossils out there still, lying quietly beneath the ground, their secrets waiting to be revealed. The story we have told is not a biography of our species, but a thriller, a mystery story; there is always something more to be discovered, a key event that changes everything, a twist in the tale. Our journey has given us some of the answers to who we are and where we came from but, for the scientists who patiently sift through the fragments of our past, the mystery tour continues.

Index

Acknowledgements

Many individuals have contributed to the television series *Walking With Cavemen* and towards compiling the story that makes up this book, and the authors would like to thank all those who have generously given of their time and expertise. We owe a special debt of gratitude to the BBC Science production team for their inspiration and creative skill in reconstructing the key steps in our evolutionary past. And particular thanks are due to the researchers and producers: Lucy Bailey, Zoe Elliot, Nick Green, Mark Hedgecoe, Claire Imber and Peter Oxley, who all diligently reviewed our manuscript – although we retain responsibility for any errors that remain. In addition, Louise would like to thank Parry, Mina and, most of all, Peter for their tolerance at being forced to walk with cavemen all summer, and John would like to thank his family – Ewa, Christopher and Toby – for their unflagging patience and encouragement.

Picture Credits

Alan Walker: 99.

American Museum of Natural History: 37 (left).

Ancient Art and Architecture Collection Ltd: 215, 217 (both).

BBC: 161 (all), 174/5, 195/6, 199 (both).

David Gur: 1, 2/3, 4 (top left, top right, bottom left), 7, 9, 10, 11, 12, 13, 16/17, 18, 19, 20, 21 (both), 22, 24/25, 26, 27, 30, 31, 32, 33, 34, 35, 39, 40, 41, 42, 43, 47, 48, 53, 55, 58/59, 61, 62, 65, 66/67, 68, 69, 71, 72, 73, 77, 78, 80, 81, 82, 83 (both), 87, 88, 89, 90, 91 (both), 92/93, 94 (both), 95, 96, 97 (both), 100, 101, 103, 104, 106 (all), 107, 110, 111 (both), 112, 113, 114, 118/9, 120, 123, 127, 129, 132, 133, 136, 137, 138/9, 141, 144, 147, 149, 150, 151/2, 159, 164, 167, 171, 172/3 (all), 178, 187, 188/9, 191 (top), 206, 208, 210, 211, 212, 219.

Hardlines: 15, 28, 36, 84, 108, 109, 143, 156 (bottom), 205.

John Reader/Science Photo Library: 29, 37 (right), 44 (both), 45, 50, 75 (left, middle), 131 (middle), 142, 157.

Madrid Scientific Films: 176, 177.

Martin Land/Science Photo Library: 131 (right).

M.P.F.T.: 56, 57.

Peter Georgi: 4 (bottom right), 14, 38, 70, 79, 86, 105, 115, 121, 122, 126, 135, 140, 145, 148, 155, 158, 160 (all), 168/9, 180, 184, 185, 190, 191 (bottom), 192, 193, 194, 200, 201, 202, 203, 218.

Renee Lynn/Science Photo Library: 85.

The Natural History Museum, London: 75 (top right, bottom right), 117 (both), 131, 156 (top), 162, 163 (both), 216.

University College London: 183 (both).

Volker Steger/Nordstar 4 Million Years of Man/Science Photo Library: 51, 125, 204.